Praise for
LEADING AND LOVING IT

"My friends Lori Wilhite and Brandi Wilson have crafted a book that is real and relevant. As a pastor's wife, I know the joys and struggles of ministry. LEADING AND LOVING IT is an amazing resource that will challenge you, guide you, and encourage you on your journey in ministry."

— Holly Furtick, wife of Steven Furtick,
pastor of Elevation Church

"As someone who's been involved with ministry for over twenty-five years, I can honestly say that pastors' wives are the lifeblood of the church. This resource will help women along the way who are struggling in the journey or need encouragement in their current season. I'm so proud of Lori and Brandi for their courage, passion, and heart for leaders in ministry!"

— Christine Caine, director of Equip & Empower Ministries and founder of The A21 Campaign

"If ever there were two leaders who can speak truth, life, love, and encouragement into the hearts of pastors' wives and women in leadership, it's Lori and

Brandi. Their gut honest stories make them authentic. Their struggles make them trustworthy. Their wisdom makes them a must-read. Hands down, if you buy a ministry leadership book this year, it should be LEADING AND LOVING IT."

—Lysa TerKeurst, *New York Times* bestselling author
of *Made to Crave* and *Unglued*

"Few things in life are as rewarding as leading in ministry, though it's also one of the most challenging things we can do. Great leaders understand how to navigate the challenges and discover the rewarding experiences God has on the other side. In LEADING AND LOVING IT, my friends Lori Wilhite and Brandi Wilson confront the challenges that all leaders face. They don't hold back, but instead allow us the opportunity to embrace—and overcome—these challenges. No matter where you lead, this book will help you experience more than the calling to lead; you'll discover the joy of fulfilling what God has empowered you to do!"

—Lisa Young, founder of the women's ministry
Flavour, and wife of Ed Young,
senior pastor of Fellowship Church

"In LEADING AND LOVING IT, Brandi and Lori provide honest insight into ten key factors unique to ministry life for women with refreshing authenticity, scriptural truths, and personal stories. As pastors' wives and women in ministry, you need to shatter your façade, come off the ministry pedestal, and open the deepest parts of your heart with Brandi and Lori so that you can live in Christ's freedom to be the best you that God uniquely created only you to be, so that you absolutely can be leading and (truly) loving it!"

—Lucretia Noble, wife of Perry Noble,
senior pastor of Newspring Church

"This book is filled with truth that will set you FREE! Lori and Brandi have a unique gift in which they are able to reveal real-life confessions with candor and discuss Christ's response to our challenges in ministry, all while encouraging us and making us laugh at the same time! This is a must-read for every woman in ministry who has ever thought she was alone on this journey!"

—Tara Jenkins, EdD, founder of Ministry Mates, Ltd., and senior pastor's wife of Fellowship Chicago

"This book is a must-read for every woman in leadership. Their authenticity will draw you in, and their stories will keep you there. There are revelations to be discovered in every chapter. This is a book to savor and a book to share with those in your leadership circle."

—Lora Batterson, wife of Mark Batterson, lead pastor of National Community Church

Leading and Loving It

Encouragement for Pastors' Wives and Women in Leadership

LORI WILHITE AND BRANDI WILSON

With a Foreword by Kay Warren

FaithWords

New York Boston Nashville

Unless otherwise indicated, all Scripture quotations are taken from the Holy Bible, New Living Translation, copyright © 1996, 2004, 2007 by Tyndale House Foundation. Used by permission of Tyndale House Publishers, Inc., Carol Stream, Illinois 60188. All rights reserved.

Scriptures taken from the Holy Bible, New International Version®, NIV®. Copyright © 1973, 1978, 1984, 2011 by Biblica, Inc.™ Used by permission of Zondervan. All rights reserved worldwide.www.zondervan.com. The "NIV" and "New International Version" are trademarks registered in the United States Patent and Trademark Office by Biblica, Inc.™

Scripture quotations from *THE MESSAGE*. Copyright © by Eugene H. Peterson 1993, 1994, 1995, 1996, 2000, 2001, 2002. Used by permission of NavPress Publishing Group.

Scriptures taken from the Holy Bible, New International Reader's Version®, NIrV® Copyright © 1995, 1996, 1998 by Biblica, Inc.™ Used by permission of Zondervan. www.zondervan.com. The "NIrV" and "New International Reader's Version" are trademarks registered in the United States Patent and Trademark Office by Biblica, Inc.™

FaithWords
Hachette Book Group
237 Park Avenue
New York, NY 10017

www.faithwords.com

Printed in the United States of America

RRD-C

First Edition: August 2013

10 9 8 7 6 5 4 3 2 1

FaithWords is a division of Hachette Book Group, Inc.

The FaithWords name and logo are trademarks of Hachette Book Group, Inc.

The Hachette Speakers Bureau provides a wide range of authors for speaking events. To find out more, go to www.hachettespeakersbureau.com or call (866) 376-6591.

The publisher is not responsible for websites (or their content) that are not owned by the publisher.

Library of Congress Cataloging-in-Publication Data
Wilhite, Lori.
 Leading and loving it : encouragement for pastors' wives and women in leadership / Lori Wilhite and Brandi Wilson.
      pages cm
Includes bibliographical references.
 ISBN 978-1-4555-2279-8 (trade pbk.) -- ISBN 978-1-4555-2278-1
(ebook) 1. Christian leadership. 2. Leadership--Religious aspects--Christianity.
3. Women in church work. 4. Spouses of clergy. 5. Wives. I. Title.
BV652.1.W487 2013
253--dc23
                              2013004652

To the Leading and Loving It community
For your inspiration, friendship, and
encouragement.
We love serving God alongside you.

CONTENTS

Acknowledgments

HAVING WATCHED OUR husbands write many books over the years, we thought we knew what we were signing up for when this book project first lifted off the ground. We really had no idea what a team effort it would be. Without the continued encouragement and pushing from so many incredible people in our lives, it would never have come to fruition.

Thanks to our amazing agent, Esther Fedorkevich. From our first conversation, your passion for this project has been unmatched. Thank you for believing in us when we weren't even sure we believed in ourselves. Happy you are part of the pastors' wives club.

From seaside dinners to late-night chat sessions, we couldn't have asked for a better editor than Jana Burson. We appreciate not only your insight but also your fun sense of humor. Glad we talked you into watching all our favorite TV shows. You are much more than an editor to us; we cherish your friendship.

Thank you to the team at Hachette for taking a chance on us—unknown and unproven. Thanks for caring enough about women in leadership to support this book and see it to completion.

Our Leading and Loving It team and sweet friends Tiffany Cooper, Jessica Cornelius, and Lisa Hughes: How incredible is it that God lets us work together even though we are separated by thousands of miles?! We can't convey how much we love our phone calls, video chats, texts, DMs, and trips. You are lifelines, and we can't imagine this life in ministry without your friendship. Glad we are Nacho Average Pastors' Wives together. And to our virtual community group leaders and our L&L It local leaders, thanks for your hearts to love and support other pastors' wives and women in ministry like you. Leading and Loving It would not be what it is without you.

Thanks to Stacy Gann, Eleana Garza, Joy Henderson, Laura Lasky, Tricia Lovejoy, Michelle Meeks, Heather Palacios, Makeda Pennycooke, Kimberly Scott, Cindy Beall, and Natalie Witcher for taking the time to dive into this book, providing not only meaningful feedback but loads of encouragement as well.

To our church families and staff at Central and Cross Point: Thank you for giving us the grace and freedom to be ourselves. It is truly a joy to serve Christ with you.

From Lori: Mom and Dad, I could not have had better role models either in spiritual life or in family life. Thanks for helping shape me into who I am today. My precious Emma and Ethan: I'm so grateful that God let me be your mom. Our prayer is that the blessing we pray over you every night will be real and tangible all the days of your lives. And my amazing husband, Jud: if you asked, I'd agree to be your "date for life" all over again. No one makes me laugh like you do. Love you, babe.

From Brandi: There is no way I could have written one word of this book without Morgantown Community Church in Kentucky, the church that accepted me as its pastor's wife at the wee age of twenty-one. Thank you to my parents, who have always been supportive and full of love. Sue, thank you for your willingness to help, your support and encouragement. My Nashville community: you give me laughter, wipe my tears, and keep life full of fun. Jett, Gage, and Brewer, my heart swells with pride for each of you. Never stop chasing after His heart. And Pete, life together has been better than I ever could have imagined. Thank you for loving me so well. Sneaking out and meeting you under that big oak tree at WKU was the best decision I ever made.

Jesus: thank you seems like so little, but we are forever grateful.

Foreword

I GREW UP in a pastor's home and, for the most part, I loved it! Some of you might say I was completely nuts, but I can truthfully say that when I saw my mom and dad be an integral part of transformation in the lives of spiritually hungry people, love people extravagantly—there for them in the Kodak moments of life as well as their deepest grief—leave an impact on generations following behind them, and partner with the God of the universe in building His church, I knew this was the life I wanted. What could possibly be better than that?

And then I married a pastor.

Being a pastor's wife was not nearly as easy as *watching* my mom be a pastor's wife! She made it seem so easy! Once I married Rick, I got a good dose of reality—too many late nights, gossipy people who seemed to enjoy my mistakes, a phone that rang off the hook, meetings ad infinitum, never enough money, volunteers who didn't show up, a husband who was cranky on Monday mornings, et cetera, et cetera, et cetera.

I needed help *fast*, and there wasn't much available. I longed for a practical guide to Ministry 101.

Two of my favorite young leaders, Lori Wilhite and Brandi Wilson, have written that book! *Leading and Loving It* is a fun, challenging, and comforting book for women like themselves: pastors' wives. I love the way they weave their down-to-earth humor, poignant life stories, and Scriptural principles into a message for every woman who is living her life in the fishbowl of ministry. Lori and Brandi will win your heart with their authenticity and encourage your soul with their real-world approach to ministry.

—*Kay Warren, cofounder of Saddleback Church*
in Lake Forest, CA

Introduction

I wouldn't mind a tummy tuck. Things have
gone south, ifyouknowwhatimean. Just sayin'.

Confession

IT ALL STARTED lighthearted and funny but in the end
turned heartbreaking. A simple blog post, requesting
confessions.

One day we set out to give pastors' wives and women
in ministry the opportunity to share their confessions.
The silly things that make them not-so-average women
in leadership. The serious struggles that had them in
full-blown choke holds. They could, and did, share
everything.

It started with an "I read vampire books, and I like
them" from Lori, and this is a snippet of what followed:

I like to wear slightly tight jeans with my very red heels.

I suffer from C.H.A.O.S. (Can't Have Anyone Over Syndrome). My house is REVOLTING.

I'm bold and nosy, but I don't really want to know about people's menstrual cycles.

I avoid the lobby. It's a hot mess.

I hate that my husband's job dictates all my friends.

I sometimes just want to skip church entirely. For a few months.

I hate having our salary supplied by church members and family. It makes me feel like I cannot spend my money however I want.

I think it is crazy weird that not only do people drive by our house to "see what we're doing" but even stranger that they tell us they do it!

I resent the way that church people make my husband and me feel insecure and inadequate.

After feeling like I could never really be honest about where I was with the Lord (we are supposed to be perfect, right?), the stress of life broke me in more ways than I care to admit. Now? I feel like I have nothing to give and live under shame of past sin and heartbreak. My confession: 1. Unworthy of being a pastor's wife. 2. I'm selfish. 3. I'm holding on by a thread.

I am DONE with ministry within the church.

Such hurt. Such heartache.

Whether you are a pastor, are a ministry wife, work on a church staff, are a missionary, serve at a nonprofit organization, or teach a Bible study, you are a leader. And to some degree, you will experience the incredible joys and painful sorrows of leadership. We get a front-row seat from which to watch how God is completely transforming people's lives, and then can be so wounded when those same people turn to us and hurl words of criticism. We are surrounded by people, yet locked away in loneliness and isolation. That's leadership.

In all the years we two, Lori and Brandi, have spent as pastors' wives, we have certainly experienced our ups and downs. Amazing highs and dark, ugly lows. We have enjoyed seasons feeling like pigtailed little girls with their jeans rolled up, splashing and playing in the ocean. We've also shuffled through bone-dry deserts, barely able to lift our feet from the hardened, cracked ground. Good times. Bad times. That has been our ministry experience. Shoot...that's life, right?

We all know how much fun it is to spread good news. When In-N-Out Burger opened its first two restaurants in Texas in May 2011, mass hysteria ensued. If you are unfamiliar with the most fabulous burger joint on the West Coast, let us educate you. There are three items on the menu: burger, cheeseburger, Double-Double. That's it. No chicken nuggets. No side salads. No snack wraps or chicken sandwiches. Sure, you can get fresh-cut fries and the best pink lemonade on the planet, but that's about it. When In-N-Out opened its doors in the Dallas area that May morning, people had spent the night in their lawn chairs, and the drive-thru line at times was over three hours long.

Now, we are huge fans, but we are talking about burgers here, people. Burgers. People sleeping on sidewalks and shaving stubbled cheeks in their cars so they could get a burger. They were that excited.

How much more should we in leadership love and embrace the work that God calls us to do? How much more excited should we be about the call of God to ministry and the privilege of serving Him there? How much more enthusiastically should we share His good news and love?

Our goal in this book is to address the challenges of leadership—sometimes small and other times stifling—wrestling with them so they do not over-whelm, drag us down, and downright steal the joy of serving Christ in ministry. We have identified, through our interaction with pastors' wives and women in ministry, ten challenges that leaders face. No matter your role; your church style; your min-istry size, denomination, or location, there are uni-versal struggles that confront most leaders at one time or another. As we look at topics like relationships, criticism, discouragement, and balance, our hope is that each of us will embrace whatever influence, ministry, and leadership God has entrusted to us...and grow to love it.

Leading and Loving It

CHAPTER 1

Influence

> If I am out and see someone from church, I
> will turn the other way/duck down another
> aisle/completely turn around to avoid them.
>
> *Confession*

FOLLOW THE LEADER

LEADERSHIP IS A funny thing. When we were kids,
there was little better than being at the head of the
pack when playing Follow the Leader. The leader got
to say which bushes to jump over, decided the best
time to do the crab walk, and created the toughest ob-
stacles possible in the confines of her backyard. But as
we grew older, leadership became scary, and we became hesitant to identify ourselves as leaders.

Along with an amazing team of women, the two of
us lead a ministry called Leading and Loving It. We've
been asked about the name tons of times, since apparently many women get a little squirmy when referred

to as leaders. As we searched for a place to connect with other pastors' wives, we couldn't think of a better description of how we wanted to live our lives.

Some people wonder...why *leading*? *Leading* is sometimes a freaky word. People shy away from being called leaders. Facilitators? Maybe. Coordinators? Sure. Leaders? Yikes! But that is what we are—leaders. Even if we didn't ask for it or plan it, we are leaders.

Some of you feel strongly called to leadership and ministry by God. You can remember all the details and circumstances preceding your acceptance of God's call on your life. Others of you find yourselves in what we call leadership by default. You married an accountant turned pastor and are now knee deep in leadership you never envisioned. Maybe you said repeatedly that you'd *never* marry someone in ministry, yet here you are...leading by default.

Then there's the other side of leading by default. Some of you knew you were marrying into a life of ministry. You were excited about your role as a pastor's wife. However, you're well aware you don't possess the gift of leadership—yet you're married to a very gifted leader. Just being married to a pastor puts you in a position of leadership and gives you influence over many people's lives. You find yourself feeling misplaced and confused by what ministry looks like for you.

No matter which case rings true in your life, you

are leading. You have an impact on the lives of your church family and ministry. They are watching. In fact, see what Paul says to believers in Hebrews 13:7: *Remember your leaders, who spoke the word of God to you. Consider the outcome of their way of life and imitate their faith.*[1]

Imitate their faith. In the Las Vegas Valley, where I (Lori) live, imitation abounds. You can visit the top of the half-scale replica of the Eiffel Tower. You can overlook a City of Light without the transcontinental flight. Under beautiful cloudy painted skies, you can take an indoor gondola ride and be serenaded by a gal with a lovely Italian accent who recently arrived from Akron, Ohio. Elvis can do your wedding, skydive into your party, or take a picture with you at the famous WELCOME TO FABULOUS LAS VEGAS sign. Between the impersonators and the wax museum, you can get your picture made with fake-famous people all over Vegas. It is a little strange.

A while ago, I was sitting at the Taco Bell drive-thru window, and the guy with the headset said, "You look like that girl in *Pulp Fiction*. I'm sorry... I'm so sorry. You do, but I'm sorry." Then he smiled a big, toothy grin and handed me our sack of burritos.

I wasn't exactly sure what to make of his declaration. I sat for a moment trying to figure out if this was some sort of strange compliment or a straight-up insult. I couldn't decide if he was apologizing to me or Uma, but either way he was apologizing—profusely. I think it must be my black bobbed hair or the *Pulp Fiction* dance that I obviously would be amazing at. Obviously.

Here we look at this verse indicating a similar thing—not the fake Christina Aguileras and fake Michael Jacksons from the Strip, but Paul is telling believers to look at us, the leadership, and imitate our lives and our faith. That is a heavy responsibility God has entrusted to us. It is much more than the lookalikes the Taco Bell guy was referring to; it is what Paul says in 1 Corinthians 11:1: *You should imitate me, just as I imitate Christ.*

FOLLOWING CHRIST

If we are going to lead with influence in the lives of people, we've got to first make sure that we are following Christ, imitating Him. While whole books can and have been written on this subject, we're going to look at just a few ways in which we need to imitate Christ.

Be consistent in your own personal devotion and spiritual growth. This is sometimes one of those tricky areas for those of us in ministry. The question isn't *What do we do?* We know what to do. We've heard or taught dozens of lessons on this very subject. We know we need to be reading the Word and tucking it in our hearts. We know we need to be pulling away for intimate time with God, developing and deepening that relationship.

The real question is *Are we doing what we already know we should do?*

If you lead the children's ministry, chances are you might not have been to "big church" in years. You've been doing the vital job of teaching children how much Jesus loves them and what the Bible has to say about their lives and choices, but you haven't sat under the teaching of God's Word in what seems like ages. If you teach a Bible study group or Sunday school class, you've certainly read your Bible, commentaries, books, and more while preparing your lessons. But when was the last time you cracked open Scripture because you thirsted for God and what He has to say to you?

We live in an incredible time of accessibility. Between Bible apps, sermon podcasts, and e-books, so much is available at our fingertips. Will we take hold of the responsibility for our own spiritual growth? Will we follow Jesus in this area of our lives?

Maybe more than anything else, you just need some alone time with your Creator. A friend of ours curls up in her big rocking chair, closes her eyes, and pretends she's laying her head on God's shoulder while she talks to Him. Do you need to curl up in your Father's lap, thanking Him, praising Him, talking to Him, listening to Him? Everything else we do in life and leadership will flow out of this intimate connection with the Lord.

Serve well. We are all quite well versed in the fact that Jesus was a servant. We see Him helping people, healing the multitude, and washing the dusty feet of His disciples. He served God; He served others. Just look at a few references right out of Acts:

Acts 3:13: *the God of all our ancestors—who has brought glory to his servant Jesus*
Acts 3:26: *God raised up his servant, Jesus*
Acts 4:30: *through the name of your holy servant Jesus*

Sometimes we are tempted in leadership to feel as if serving is nothing more than a sacrifice. We serve because we love God and know He has called us to serve, but our hearts feel little more than duty bound. We see serving as labor rather than loving God and loving others.

Remember the royal wedding of Prince William and Kate Middleton in 2011? What a fantastic spectacle! Two billion onlookers. Handsome military dress uniforms. A horse-drawn carriage. A powerhouse guest list of athletes, actors, musicians, and world leaders. And those outrageous hats. Who could forget the hats? Everyone asked to serve the Royal Family that day must have been absolutely thrilled. What an incredible honor! (Although someone really should have stopped Prince Andrew's daughter from wearing that awful tan bow/hat contraption.)

That is why our sweet friend Jessica Cornelius, a senior pastor's wife, says, "When you are commissioned by an earthly king to do something for him, it is an honor. Why, then, is being commissioned by our Heavenly King considered a sacrifice?"[2] Wow.

In order to view serving as the privilege it is, we must serve out of the overflow of our hearts. Serving out of our own strength, our own power, our own energy won't get us very far. Have you ever been in one of those pedal boats out on the lake? You quickly spin your feet, kind of like Fred Flintstone and Barney Rubble in their foot-powered car. Your feet move, but somehow that boat barely budges. The waves push against you, and your kid in the passenger seat is no help whatsoever. You need a motor, an outside force, to propel you forward. Like everything else in our lives and leadership, serving must be done through the power and strength of Jesus Christ.

When we are consistent in that first part of following Jesus, growing in our relationship with God, then Paul's plea in 1 Thessalonians, *And may the Master pour on the love so it fills your lives and splashes over on everyone around you,*[3] can come to fruition as we serve the people God places in our lives. You gain the ability to serve out of a pure desire and fulfillment of purpose.

Be moved by compassion. On occasion, you might hear southern women like us say "I don't give a hoot." This is the very kind way a sweet-tea-drinking southern gal might communicate "I don't care." All leaders have, somewhere in the back of our minds, what we lovingly refer to as a give-a-hooter. You know, that part of us that cares deeply about people. The part that happily stands, listens, and prays for someone in the lobby. But sadly, sometimes our give-a-hooters break. Maybe we've overstuffed our schedules and stretched ourselves too thin, maybe we're totally depleted and haven't let Christ fill us back up, or maybe we've been deeply wounded by a group of people in our ministries. No matter the reason, sometimes we find ourselves with broken give-a-hooters.

You see a lady from Bible study at Target, and you quickly push that bulky red cart down another aisle. Service ends, people make a beeline for you, and you quickly duck down the back hallway. If we are brutally honest with ourselves, we've probably all been there at one point or another.

Let's look at Jesus in Matthew 14. Jesus has been teaching and healing, healing and teaching. He's ministering to people at every turn. The crowds are constantly following Him when He hears that John the Baptist has been beheaded, his head literally served up on a platter for Herod's wife and her daughter. In verse 13, the Bible says: *As soon as Jesus heard the news,*

He left in a boat to a remote area to be alone. Obviously up-set and needing time alone with God, His friends, and His emotions, Jesus hops into a boat and heads to an out-of-the-way location.

We can imagine that Jesus must have been weary, both emotionally and physically. He could really have used some time alone, but the crowds heard where he was headed and followed Him.

As His boat docked, Jesus was probably looking forward to a peaceful, quiet time. Instead, He locked eyes with a huge crowd as He stepped from the boat. The Bible doesn't say He threw up His hands, wondering what was wrong with those people. It doesn't say that He turned and tried to find a hiding place on that little boat. It doesn't say that He heaved a great sigh and rolled His eyes. No. The Scripture says, in verse 14: *Jesus saw the huge crowd as He stepped from the boat, and He had compassion on them and healed their sick.*

By far, the most recorded emotional response of Jesus is compassion.[4] And if we are going to follow and imitate Jesus, then we have to take a long, hard look at ourselves in the mirror and ask, "What emotional response most moves me when I look at people?"

When we see the line of people waiting to talk to us after service, are we moved by frustration? When we look at the couple who sent a nasty e-mail to our husband, are we moved by anger? When we see the woman who has been gossiping about our family, are we moved by bitterness?

Or are we, instead, moved by compassion, empathy, grace, and mercy?

Remember, as with everything else we do in life and leadership, compassion will flow out of our intimate connection with the Lord. If you feel as if your give-a-hooter is broken, spend some time with Christ. Pray for the ability to see the people in your ministry with the same eyes He does. Ask Him to ignite a deep love for His children in your heart and life. Seek a renewed compassion for the people He has called you to serve.

FOLLOW ME

As we are following Christ, it is quite likely that, as influencers, we are being followed as well. Remember that verse in Hebrews? Paul says, *Remember your leaders....Consider the outcome of their way of life and imitate their faith.* God has put you in a position of influence. Whether you asked for it or not, whether you are comfortable with it or not, you are a leader and influencer. The ladies in your Bible study are watching; the kids in your youth group are paying attention. You may be the topic of Sunday lunch conversation, and a great subject for office water cooler discussions. What then, are we going to do about that?

One of our favorite leadership passages is 1 Timothy 4:12: *Teach believers with your life: by word, by demeanor, by love, by faith, by integrity.*[5] If we are going to be the kinds of leaders God has called us to be, then it is vitally important that we be willing to lead with our entire lives. Let's look at teaching people through our words, attitudes, and actions.

Lead by word. Words are powerful little things. They have the power to lift people up to great heights or to tear them down to the bone. Words can bring incredible warmth and encouragement or can totally destroy people. With just a few well-chosen words, we can protect the unity of our churches and staffs; or with just a few ill-spoken words, we can drive a giant wedge between staff members and plant seeds of disunity in our churches and organizations. When we hear gossip and negativity, we can either lovingly yet firmly shut them down, or we can stoke the fire with our participation. We can highlight the incredible things that God is doing in our ministries to friends and family, or we can use those people we love as sounding boards for the negativity and hurt we are feeling about a work situation. We are, as 1Timothy says, teaching others with our words. Let's be intentional about making them the kinds of words that bring life, encouragement, unity, and affirmation.

My (Brandi's) middle son, Gage, provides a perfect example of using words to edify and bring life. His ability to use words as a positive influence is a God-given gift that flowed out of him at a very young age and without any prompting. He was about four the first time I remember him commenting on something I was wearing. Pete and I were heading out on a date night. When I walked downstairs not wearing yoga pants and a tank top, Gage immediately took notice. "Momma, you look so pretty. You're going to have a lot of fun tonight." More recently at dinner my oldest son, Jett, described a school situation in which his feelings had been hurt. Gage immediately responded with "Jett, I'm sorry your feelings were hurt, but I think you're really fun to hang out with." I can't tell you the number of times Gage has changed the atmosphere of a family situation with a few loving, well-spoken words. Our words have that same power.

Lead by attitude. Like our words, our attitudes and demeanor make a huge impact on those in our circle of influence. Sometimes our attitudes can speak as loudly as any words we could offer up. A well-timed sigh or eye roll doesn't need any accompanying words to clearly get the point across. We all took wonderful advantage of this during our teenage years, much to our mothers' displeasure. We can speak volumes without ever uttering a word. Leading people through our attitudes is incredibly powerful.

Lead by action. Lead by example. Little is more powerful than leading by example. Our actions truly do speak louder than words. One night, curled up in bed with my (Lori's) precious eleven-year-old daughter, Emma, I reminded her, as I often do, that she is incredibly lucky to have cool parents. Not everyone gets to have cool parents, you know. She giggled and thought I was silly as I listed all the supercool things about her dad and me. Suddenly she chimed in, saying, "We are kind of like a superfamily, with superpowers."

According to Emma, here are our superpowers (announced in the dramatic, deep voice used in movie trailers):

Daddy: with the power to use the good words of the Bible to beat the bad guys.

Emma: with the power of cuteness. When the bad guys faint due to her supercuteness, they can be defeated.

Ethan: with the power of imagination. Anything he can imagine can really happen.

Roxy (our bulldog): with the power of laser-beam eyes.

Then Emma paused and so sweetly looked at me and said, "Mom, what can your superpower be?"

I was uncertain, but with that amazing lineup of superpowers, it was sure to be a doozy. Then she dropped it on me.

Mom: with the power of bad cooking and the ability to food-poison the bad guys.

Now, that, my friends, deserves a high five for hilarity! While I have been told I am the best peanut butter and jelly sandwich maker ever, I am obviously no Rachael Ray! My actions and example in the kitchen are nothing to brag about.

There are actions that matter even more than my lack of culinary skill and examples that are being watched by more than my hungry kids. Every day, we lead through our actions, large and small. We lead through our generosity to others and our sharing of our personal struggles. We lead by stopping in the middle of a jammed hallway to pray for someone and by taking a newcomer's arm to show him or her around the church. We lead by example when we are the first to follow through on something being asked from the platforms of our churches and when we remember to check on the sick wife of a volunteer. Yes, our strongest leadership is seen in the activity of our daily lives.

When we can grow to a place of leading through our words, attitude, and actions, we are well on our way to leading with our entire lives.

AUTHENTICITY VS TRANSPARENCY

Ministry and leadership are at times referred to as the fishbowl, the glass house, and the spotlight. It can be very tempting to alter our public lives under the scrutiny of hundreds of eyes, but our public lives need to be a representation of what is going on in our private lives. While we live incredibly public lives, we have the right to have private lives as well. People may check out the contents of our grocery carts at the store, turn their chairs to join us at dinner in restaurants, or want to know who we use as a plumber, hairdresser, or dentist. That is why *authenticity* and *transparency* have become such hot-topic words in leadership.

While authenticity and transparency are often talked about simultaneously, they are really quite different. Authenticity is you being genuinely you no matter the location, situation, or audience. It is you being the same real you in the aisles at Target, at Bible study on Thursday morning, during the PTA meeting, at the seventh-grade girls' discipleship group, at your eight-year-old's soccer games, and in the church lobby on Sunday morning. No masks. No fakery. No phoniness. Just you being the imperfect yet uniquely gifted person you are.

However, transparency is something else. Being transparent is being completely see-through. This is allowing people into the deeply personal, private side of your life, sharing your intimate struggles and celebrations, challenges and victories. It's not necessary to be completely transparent with everyone, but we absolutely *must* be transparent with a few someones. As Kay Warren has reminded us: people in ministry have a right to a private life. We do not, however, have the right to private sin.[6] We have to allow people into the very private side of our lives because accountability is only as good as the transparency and trust you are able to bring into a few relationships.

What does this difference look like as it is played out in leadership? We love these examples shared by Linda Seidler, a church planter's wife:

Authentic: "Our marriage is not perfect, and we have many challenges."

Transparent: "We were arguing last night, and I threw a dish over his head through the window."

Authentic: "It has not always been easy raising our children."

Transparent: "My daughter has been struggling for the past year with anorexia and bulimia."

Authentic: "My morning was a little stressful and hectic today."

Transparent: "The checking account was overdrawn, and the bills are not getting paid."

Authentic: "Please pray for me this week."

Transparent: "My depression is overwhelming, and I can't get out of bed."[7]

Not being completely transparent with every person you lock eyes with doesn't mean you are inauthentic. It does mean you are protecting part of your private life, and you certainly have that right. But be careful to always be authentically you, because our public lives should always be a reflection of our private lives.

SOCIAL NETWORKING: WHERE PUBLIC AND PRIVATE WORLDS MEET

There are few places where our private and public worlds crash and clash more than the social networking realm. Aaahh. Social networking. A wonderful little tool of connection and encouragement and a strange little weapon at times. When we talk to women in leadership, questions about social networking always come up. Do we "friend" all our church members on Facebook? Do we "unfriend" people? How do we manage different social networking and blogging issues? Here is a little practical insight into our online lives:

Our online home. We treat our teeny-tiny corners of the social networking world like our online homes. So if we wouldn't let people standing in our kitchens talk to us about our friends, our churches, or our families the way they are talking to us online, then we delete, block, or unfriend. We don't mind people disagreeing with us at all. We are quite aware that we are far from having all the right answers, but when people are hateful or just plain rude, well, we don't have time for that. And we're willing to bet, neither do you.

We have friends who feel as if they can't delete people online because they want to keep an eye on what's being said about them. Not us. Ignorance is bliss. We don't get upset, anxious, or angry about what we don't see. So we just remove it.

Social networking is more like a billboard than a diary. We need to assume that nothing is private. With the ability to copy, download, share, and repost, we decided long ago that if we wouldn't post our update on a billboard in town or on the screens in our churches, we wouldn't post it on Facebook. That means (although we've certainly had our moments) no whining, no grouching, and no oversharing... #ifyouknowwhatimean.

We don't consider Facebook, Twitter, and Instagram part of our private lives, but an extension of our public lives. So we've always followed and friended just about everyone. Old friends from our third-grade T-ball team? Yes. Church members? Yes. The PTA moms at school? Yes. Random people that we don't know where in the world they've come from? Yes.

Because our private worlds are separate from our online worlds, we don't worry too much about who's looping into our social networking lives. While we're sure that doesn't work for everyone, it works for us.

It's not a boxing ring. Confrontations with people on Twitter and Facebook are completely useless. As our friend Linda says, "A disparaging dialogue [on social networking] accomplishes nothing and will never have a positive outcome, so I choose not to participate, even when I am attacked head-on." Sure, you can always address that kind of trouble in face-to-face sit-downs or over the phone, but it's best not to use Facebook like a public boxing ring for disagreements.

It is important to remember the other side of that coin as well. It isn't just about responding to confrontation, it's important not to dish it out, either.

When my (Lori's) kids were little, they absolutely loved the oh-so-popular *Yo Gabba Gabba!* I, however, did not share their enthusiasm for DJ Lance and having a party in my tummy. With an overflowing laundry basket in front of me and the sounds of *Yo Gabba Gabba!* bouncing off the walls of our family room, I shot out this snarky little tweet: "Folding laundry to the sounds of *Yo Gabba Gabba!* Two things that make me cringe."

I set my phone down with a little smile at my self-dubbed wittiness and started folding pj's. About ten minutes later, I got this tweet back from the creators of *Yo Gabba Gabba!:* "Make you cringe? Sorry. We're just trying to make magic for the children."

Oh, crud. Can you say #fail?

I quickly responded with an embarrassed "I'm so sorry. My kids totally love your show!"

Fast-forward ten more minutes to this tweet from one of our staff wives, who apparently *knows* the creators of the show: "That's our senior pastor's wife. Don't worry, we'll win her over to the fan club."

You've. Got. To. Be. Kidding. Me. What are the odds? That's when I realized I had a remarkable ability to stick my big, fat virtual foot in my mouth. Maybe, just maybe, I needed to keep my snarky, negative feelings to myself.

Social networking is really not the platform for airing complaints about someone else. Remember, people are reading every word you type with your thumbs and seeing every photo you upload. Make sure to lead online as well.

Now let's get back to that original question asked at the beginning of this chapter: Why *leading*? Whether in our online lives or in our daily lives and routines, God has given us an incredible responsibility and gift of influence in the lives of others as pastors' wives and women in leadership.

Still other people wonder…why *Loving It*? Leading is tough. It is pressure filled. Expectations abound. Hurt happens. If we're honest, we've certainly had our moments, and our longer periods, when we didn't love it. In fact, we've had times when we were really just trying to survive. But there are also blessings. So many incredible blessings. We are leading as followers of Jesus and loving it because it's what He's called us to.

In the end, it's Leading and Loving It because that's what we want for women in ministry and pastors' wives. It's what we want for ourselves. If we can create a community that truly encourages, connects, and equips women, helping them grow in the love of the leadership that God has called them to, then those women can have an incredible impact in their marriages, families, ministries, and communities.

As we journey through the challenges laid out in the rest of this book, that is our desire for each of you. Our prayer is that we each learn to navigate through difficulty and do not allow it to steal the joy in the calling God has on our lives. May we all grow to a place of leading and loving it.

CHAPTER 2

Expectations and the Pedestal

> I worry that if I say the wrong thing or cross
> that imaginary line, I will cost my husband his
> job.
>
> *Confession*

FROM THE OUTSIDE looking in, life for Kimberly *looked* perfect. She had five beautiful children, a charismatic and successful pastor husband, and a thriving television ministry. They had planted six growing churches and lived in one of the most fabulous cities in the country, San Diego.

But if people had been able to pull the curtain back on Kimberly's life, they would have seen a woman clinging to the top of an unsteady pedestal, ready to collapse at any moment. A pedestal is really nothing more than a top-heavy perch that can be knocked over with either a jolting bump or a full-on wrecking ball. Kimberly secretly carried her own pain, carefully covering it with a shiny, lovely-looking veneer. Whether out of love, fear, or flat-out shame, she also tried to cover the weaknesses of her husband and their marriage. Not wanting to expose the vulnerability of their crumbling marriage and family, she hid anything she felt wasn't right.

You see, when you are on a pedestal, you don't have to be authentic or share your struggles with others. It feels safer to be on the pedestal instead of living with people in the midst of struggle. Fear that people would lose their faith in the Lord or faith in their leaders drove Kimberly to protect that carefully crafted public image. She did not feel she could reach out for help. She just clung to the edges of that teetering pedestal.

Kimberly was a fifth-generation pastor's wife. She grew up in a loving, stable ministry home. She was very aware of what a healthy marriage looked like; however, she fiercely guarded her husband and the situation they were in because she didn't want to divulge the truth. Her husband recognized and acknowledged her only in front of an audience. At home he was distant and rejecting, but in public he was encouraging and praising. She craved to be loved completely, not only in front of a crowd, but also in the security of her own home. From the outside, Kimberly's life was attractive, satisfying, and comfortable. But the view from the inside was dark, lonely, and agonizingly painful.

Feeling as if she was going to implode under the

pressure of keeping up appearances, she lay on the floor of her home, desperately crying out to God because she felt like such a failure. God quietly spoke to her heart: "I don't want you to look through anyone else's eyes, including your husband's, for approval. I only want you to look through My eyes and perspective and how I see you. See yourself through My reflection." That began to break the chains of a lifelong battle that had been focused on the approval of others.

The carefully crafted life and the image Kimberly and her husband had built crumbled down around them. Kimberly shockingly discovered that her husband had spent years in extramarital affairs. In fact, their entire marriage had involved more than just the two of them. Within weeks, they resigned from their ministry. In one fell swoop, Kimberly went from being a pastor's wife and a homeschooling mom to a divorced single mother of five, unemployed, on welfare, and spiritually as well as physically drained. Her husband refused to take the steps necessary to heal their marriage, and Kimberly found herself trying to pick up the pieces of an absolutely shattered life.

Expectations. We all have them. Many of us push against them. The piano-playing, be-silent-and-always-agreeable expectations of previous generations have given way to be-at-every-function, teach-all-Bible-studies, be-perfect-

and-always-happy, and lead-the-women's-ministry expectations. When we allow other people's expectations—
or even our expectations of ourselves—the power to
shape us into the kinds of women and leaders we should
be, rather than the God who called us into ministry in
the first place, we find ourselves quickly trapped in that
prison otherwise known as a pedestal. As Gloria Steinem
says, "A pedestal is as much a prison as any small, confined space."[1]

In this chapter, we're going to take a look at the
expectations of others and the effects of being placed
on a pedestal; our expectations of ourselves and our
willingness to climb up on that pedestal; and ways of
hopping down off the pedestal altogether—resting in
the person God made us to be.

THE EXPECTATIONS OF OTHERS

The pedestal is probably one of the main reasons we
often introduce ourselves at church as Lori and Brandi
and leave off our last names. We enter the world
of ladies-with-one-name . . . you know, Cher, Madonna,
Adele, Pink. That's us, minus the crazy hair and scan-
dalous outfits. Don't get us wrong. We are proud to be
married to our husbands. They don't have bigger fans
than us; we absolutely love being the wives of our guys.
But one of the first confessions we made to each other
years ago was that we have a tendency to hide out at
church. The main reason this happens is that we want

people's first impression of us to be...us. Not Pete's wife. Not Jud's wife. Not the pastor's wife. Just us.

Let's be honest: people treat you differently when you're married to the pastor. As soon as people realize who you are, their perception of you changes. They may expect you to be the perfect wife, the perfect mother, or the perfect woman in general. Lots of times they expect you to have the same gifts as your husband—to possess *his* charisma, *his* biblical knowledge, *his* magnetic personality, and *his* communication style. While no one admires these qualities in our husbands more than we do, we also know that we were created as different individuals. Honestly, most weekends we feel successful if we get to church on time, wearing shoes that actually match each other, and with our kids wearing clean clothes.

I (Brandi) think my hesitation about letting people know I was the pastor's wife started before we were even married. When Pete and I met, he was working in youth ministry and had grown a struggling small-town church youth group of about ten kids to a thriving outreach ministry with about two hundred teenagers. (I knew he had the gift of evangelism the first day I met him.) At one of our Wednesday-night services, I was leading a group of about ten teenagers after a fabulous message on salvation. One of the guys came up to me as we were ending and told me he wanted to become a Christian. The kid and I sat down, cracked open my Bible, and started reading passages from Romans together. As our discussion ended, I asked him if he was ready to pray and found my eyes filling with tears when he answered yes. It was hard to contain my excitement. This was the first person I'd led to Christ on my own. We finished praying and opened our eyes, and he looked at me and innocently asked, "Do I need to pray with Pete to make sure it took, or did you really know what you were doing?" Sweet guy didn't know my years at First Baptist Church in Fredonia, Kentucky, had more than adequately prepared me for that moment. I can openly laugh about it now, but back then it was probably the first moment when I realized that people would measure me based on my connection to my husband.

PLAY-DOH, THE ARK, AND THE NEED FOR APPROVAL

So often, the expectations we face from other people are tightly tied to our need for approval. We spend much of our time wondering and worrying about the thoughts, feelings, and approval of others.

When my (Brandi's) oldest son, Jett, was four, he had a woman named Stacy as his Cross Point Kids teacher. Stacy was an exceptional lady. She was a servant, a gifted Bible teacher, and very well respected by everyone in our growing church plant. I truly think if you looked close enough you could see the faint glimmer of Stacy's halo. She was one godly lady, and she had our sweet Jett in her class each week.

One particular weekend the lesson was on Noah's ark. Everyone knows Noah's ark, especially our kid. Heck, we'd read about Noah's ark in his *Beginner's Bible*, had sung a Noah's ark song repeatedly, and had watched a Noah's ark video many, many, many times. Jett had this lesson down...or maybe not! Class started with saintly Stacy handing a tub of Play-Doh to each child and asking them to use the clay to make one animal that might have been on the ark with Noah.

The kids went to work. They were smashing and molding, squishing and creating. Then the time came for them to share their formations. There were giraffes, elephants, dogs, and even a cheetah. Everyone was right on track; then it was Jett's turn. Stacy walked over to his table and in her angelic voice said, "Jett, I think I know what your animal is. You've rolled it out like a tube. I think you made a snake." At which point my sweet son looked up at her, giggled, and said, "No, Mrs. Stacy, I didn't make a snake; I made a penis." Oh, yes...he did! My kid, the pastor's kid, made an inappropriate object in his church class. I was shocked when Mrs. Stacy told Pete and me the story. Where did that come from? Our *Beginner's Bible* sure didn't include any unsuitable figures on Noah's ark; neither did the song we sang or the video Jett had memorized.

Looking back now, I realize I really wasn't all that

embarrassed that Jett had made an unfitting object out of Play-Doh; any mom of boys knows little boys = potty humor. I *was* embarrassed that Jett had made his questionable creation for Mrs. Stacy. What must she think? What did she say to her husband about my parenting that afternoon on the way home from church? What did she say to the ladies in the Bible study she led that week?

You know why Jett's creation bothered me so much? Because I worried too much about what people thought of me. I was driven by the internal addiction of approval—the disease to please. I'd venture to guess that many of you suffer from the same disease.

CONFESSION TIME: WE ARE PEOPLE PLEASERS

Yep, we surely are. We like people to like us. No, that probably isn't the whole truth. We *need* people to like us—that's closer to the truth. For a long, long time, this is something we've known about ourselves. It is a weakness; something that needs work.

Some lessons we are forced to relearn. Call us stubborn (or maybe we're just slow), but some lessons take a little longer to really sink in so we can live by them daily. People pleasing isn't just a weakness, not just something we should work on. Instead, it is something far more serious. It is entrapment, and it is idolatry.

Over the years we have learned that when we focus on pleasing someone else, we are actually selling ourselves to them. *By seeking their approval, we become their slaves.*[2] We live a life of entrapment rather than the life of freedom God intended us to live. The tiny prison of the pedestal traps us.

Instead of remaining under the headship of Christ, we hand over the keys to our freedom to people. The Bible says in 1 Corinthians: *God paid a high price for you, so don't be enslaved by the world.*[3]

God purposefully created us with a need *only He can meet.* It is not a need that can be met by our husbands, our children, or our friends; not by the approval of the elders, the ladies in Bible study, or the youth volunteers; not in the satisfaction of the grumpy guy in the third row or the lady who tracks us down immediately after service ends to make her opinions known. It is in Christ—only in Christ.

People pleasing is, at its worst, a form of idolatry— that's right, worshipping a big, fat, old, ugly idol. Both of us have been at the place where we were putting the thoughts and opinions of others above the Lord's. We have let the criticism or expectations of a few wreck us, even though we knew we were doing what the Lord wanted.

But no more. Nope. Almost daily, and most assuredly weekly, we have to make sure the Lord is back on the throne in that part of our lives. Will we still struggle? Definitely. But let's call it out for what it is now, in all its ugliness: the idolatry of people pleasing.

So there it is. Deep breath.

Let us, instead, cling to this: *Am I now trying to win the approval of men, or of God? Am I trying to please men? If I were still trying to please men, I would not be a servant of Christ* (Galatians 1:10).

The challenge becomes figuring out what to do with the expectations of others, and the even tougher expectations we place on ourselves.

MY TOUGHEST CRITIC IS ME

I (Lori) have very high expectations of myself. Way back in the prechildren, premarriage dating days, my husband and I had some pretty amazing but not-so-Hollywood moments (although they've always seemed quite Hollywood-like to me).

Jud asked me out the first time by telling me he wanted to buy me coffee "to encourage me." Worst. Pickup. Line. Ever. Living in cities two hours away from each other, we rolled quarters to pay for our incredibly expensive long-distance phone bills, since this was before the days of unlimited calling.

He told me he loved me for the first time in the very romantic McDonald's parking lot in the thriving metropolis of Plainview, Texas. And when Jud talked to his mentor about asking me to marry him, he was told, "Your wife will make you or break you in ministry."

That is part of our story. The how-did-you-meet-and-marry story told over a hundred dinners and at dozens of parties. It is recounted every time we meet someone new or need a good sermon illustration for a marriage series. But the part of our story that continually haunted me was: your wife could break you in ministry.

Notice, I conveniently left out of my brain the *make you* part of that statement. Instead, I became obsessed with and hampered by the knowledge that I could break my husband's ministry. It was like carrying a sixty-pound backpack while hiking up a steep hill (not that I'd know from personal experience). I felt completely weighed down.

The possibility of *breaking* my husband caused me to start building a very small, very confined little pedestal for myself. On that pedestal I felt I had to say all the right things, watching every word that came out of my mouth. I was compelled to be at every single event and lead in all the right areas. I could not be myself! *What if that wasn't good enough?* I could not share my struggles! *What if people couldn't handle it?* I sat in the tiny prison I had built, falling deeper and deeper into depression.

A few years later, I heard Kay Warren, the wife of the senior pastor at Saddleback Church in Lake Forest, California, say: "People will put you on a pedestal. We cannot control others. However, you don't have to hop up on that pedestal on your own."[4] That is exactly what I had chosen to do. I had climbed up onto that little pedestal prison all by myself. But I did not have to choose to stay there, and neither do you. Instead, you can grab hold of the person God says you are.

And God says:

You are good enough through Christ. (Romans 5:1)
You are called. (Romans 8:30)
You are God's children. (John 1:12)
You have been bought with a price, and you belong to God. (1 Corinthians 6:19–20)
You have been chosen by God and adopted as His children. (Ephesians 1:3–8)
You are assured that God works for your good in all circumstances. (Romans 8:28)
You have been established, anointed and sealed by God. (2 Corinthians 1:21–22)
You are confident that God will complete the good work He started in you. (Philippians 1:6)
You are a citizen of heaven. (Philippians 3:20)
You are God's workmanship. (Ephesians 2:10)
You can do all things through Christ, who strengthens you. (Philippians 4:13)[5]

Over several years, I had to learn to reframe my expectations of myself in light of God's Word. This was so freeing! Learning that many of our expectations cannot and should not be met liberates us from the confining prison of trying to measure up to impossible standards.

We need to learn some essential truths:

We are not omniscient. It is impossible to know all the answers, both biblically and spiritually, to all things in life, relationships, parenting, marriage, and the many struggles that come from relationships. We cannot have every line of Scripture stuffed into our heads. We cannot be the sole source of wisdom, counsel, and advice. *We are not God; neither are you. And that's a good thing.*

We are not omnipresent. We cannot be at every baby shower, wedding, surgery, hospital bed, women's ministry event, small-group party, and leadership meeting while still making it to every soccer game, school performance, PTA meeting, date night, and birthday party. It is not possible. We cannot be in all places at all times. *We are not God; neither are you. And that's a good thing.*

We are not omnipotent. It is not possible to have a life free of struggle, weakness, and heartache. We're not able to handle anything that life and people throw our way. We are not perfect. We are not all-powerful. *We are not God; neither are you. And that's a good thing.*

Realizing our own limitations and the limitless power of God enables us to hop down off those pedestals in our lives. It ensures that we elevate God to His rightful place, and that we are able to lead humbly from a place of brokenness, acknowledging our own weakness and shortcomings. It helps us drop those

crazy expectations and move forward in God's freedom.

DEAR "I'M A BAD PASTOR'S WIFE"

Recently someone found Leading and Loving It by
Googling the phrase: "I'm a bad pastor's wife." We
can't tell you how this hurt our hearts, and we wondered what made her think she was a bad pastor's wife.

Is it that she feels she can't live up to people's expectations?
We can't make everyone happy, and are bound to disappoint someone—maybe a lot of someones. There
hasn't been a pastor's wife we've encountered who has
been able to meet all of those expectations.

Is it that she can't live up to her own expectations? We can
totally relate, since we often fall short of what we feel
we should do or who we feel we should be. While regularly showing grace to other people, we're notoriously
hard on ourselves and often find it difficult to extend
that same grace to ourselves.

*Is it that she feels she falls short when comparing herself to
others?* Yep, we've been there, too, wishing we were as
good as this lady, wishing we could do as much as that
one, or wishing we were more like this other pastor's
wife. But we're not those people. Neither are you. Actually, we aren't supposed to be.

We need to grow to a place of embracing our brokenness and our shortcomings, being willing to hop
down off the pedestal and share our vulnerabilities. In

Vegas, Central Christian Church has campuses inside several prisons, including a women's correctional center. The cinder-block room fills to capacity with over three hundred inmates in their blue jumpsuits, worshipping, singing, and lifting their hands to the Lord. What is immediately noticeable is the absolute joy radiating out of those ladies. They are beaming, smiling from ear to ear.

But something else is quickly noticeable. Most of those women—many in their twenties, thirties, and forties—are missing teeth. Some have two holes in their smiles, others have four or five gaps. Apparently, when the inmates have dental problems, if it is cheaper to extract a tooth than to fix it, that tooth is pulled. It does not matter if it is one of their front teeth or not; it is pulled.

Looking out across this room, you will see women who, without shame over their gap-toothed smiles, are beaming with gratitude for the way God is moving in their lives.

That is the smile of the second chance.

While most of us are not surrounded by cinder-block prison walls, we are often trapped in these pedestal prisons of our own making or the making of others. We've been hit, hurt, dinged, and damaged along the way. At times those hurts come from others, through criticism or betrayal. At other times, they are self-inflicted wounds we carry because we feel we do not live up to expectations or somehow feel like the odd man out. We walk around trying to hide our imperfections and our shortcomings. Yes, we may smile, but we refuse to grin widely, revealing the gaps in our teeth.

The two of us believe it is time for all of us, as women and as leaders, to embrace our smile of the second chance, living joyfully and without abandon in the person God made us to be. We must know that we all have imperfections and shortcomings and not allow those to take away from the joy of smiling ear-to-ear.

God knows exactly who you are and how He made you. He has put you in this role knowing all your faults, failings, and shortcomings. He knows the gaps in your grin, and He knows you are exactly who He needs in this place, at this time. Jump off that prison pedestal and walk in the freedom of Christ.

Kimberly learned what it meant to have every expectation for her future dashed, but she learned that God had another future. She is a second chance kind of person. Four years after Kimberly's life was devastated, God lovingly and carefully put her back together. She met and married Tim, another pastor—a loving, attentive husband and a wonderful father to her five children. Tim had also experienced the life-shattering destruction of extramarital affairs on the part of his first wife. God gave Kimberly and Tim the beautiful marriage they had both dreamed of, but He did not restore their broken pedestals. Instead, He did something far greater. He gave them the courage to lead out of their brokenness and vulnerability.

Now Tim and Kimberly use the very place that used to separate them from others—the pedestal—to share their own struggles and encourage others to reach out. They use it as a way to bring safety to people, to show them God's love, grace, and mercy—the same love, grace, and mercy that put them back together again.

CHAPTER 3

Personal Calling

> I HATE being asked to head up everything
> that no other woman wants to do. Or what
> some other women think the church needs but
> will not lead.
>
> *Confession*

I (BRANDI) ALWAYS love it when Mother's Day rolls around and my children's teachers have them create acknowledgments that describe me. Like many of you, I have been identified as forty-five years older than my actual age, have been told that I am loved for my ability to microwave chicken nuggets, and have received those audacious portraits in which I have two rather large purple eyes and stringy blue hair. But I think one of my favorite Mother's Day acknowledgments happened more recently when my then eight-year-old son, Jett, christened me with "You are a famous pastor's wife."

What was so fascinating about that statement was that for years I've avoided using the term *pastor's wife* to describe myself. Sure, I'm wife, mom, child of God, daughter, daughter-in-law, friend, aunt, volunteer, cheerleader, mentor, niece, cousin, and swimsuit model (okay, maybe I threw in that last one). But my son's referring to me as a pastor's wife was fascinating because he acknowledged something in my life that I rarely acknowledged myself.

Listing *pastor's wife* or *woman in ministry* to describe ourselves makes both of us a bit uncomfortable. See, neither of us ever felt the call to ministry the way our husbands did. But we also never felt that ministry was an obligation. We enjoyed what we did, loved our churches, and felt blessed to be part of the community God placed us in. But without feeling the call our husbands had felt, we were left wondering how we "fit" in their ministries. Unfortunately, we've wasted a lot of time thinking our husbands were the ones doing the "important work." It wasn't our churches' fault; we both have a heart for the local church and readily volunteer on a regular basis. It wasn't our husbands' fault. It wasn't the fault of ministry. We now realize that it is because God never wanted us to *just FIT*. There was no contentment in *just fitting*. Just fitting means you're working around others rather than allowing God to work through you. God's greatest dream for our lives was for each of us to be exclusively who He created us to be and to serve Him and praise Him through that. God doesn't want us doing ministry in the shadow of our husbands, our ministry partners, our bosses, or anyone.

Here's where things can get tricky, regardless of your role, whether you're a pastor's wife, the children's ministry director, the administrative assistant, or the founder of a nonprofit—you can be guilty of becoming effective merely by association. We can be tempted to ride our husbands' or our ministries' spiritual coattails. God wants more for us than that.

If you're in leadership of any sort, you've probably been guilty of being "effective by association" at some point in your walk with Christ. We like to focus on John 15:8 when we're drifting into that pattern: *When you produce much fruit, you are my true disciples. This brings great glory to my Father.* As Christ's disciples, we are meant to be profoundly effective, profoundly fruit-bearing in our personal lives, not simply because we're part of a healthy, growing church. We must all ask ourselves this question: *Have I been living life only effective by association?*

We can fall into a trap of depending on our husbands' faith, our pastor's guidance, or our ministry leader's vision. Don't misunderstand us—the leadership, vision, and faith of those people are of vital importance. But their faith can't be your faith. You have to know who *you* are in Christ. Just because you're under great leadership or married to an amazing pastor, you can't let their walk with Christ be your walk with Christ. Their relationship with God cannot replace your relationship with God. Your effectiveness cannot be measured by the effectiveness of your organization, but rather must be measured by what *you* are doing to be the hands and feet of Jesus.

We love the way our friend Holly Furtick, senior pastor's wife at Elevation Church in North Carolina, described it:

> In our line of work, it is easy to fall into the trap of depending on my husband's faith. His vision, his purpose, and dangerously, his relationship with God. It's a hard line to balance. He is my husband; we are one. His vision should be my vision, his purpose mine. And he is my spiritual leader, his relationship with God directly affects mine. But his relationship with God cannot replace my own relationship with God.
>
> I also cannot ride the spiritual coat-tails of our church. It is such a privilege to be a part of a move of God. There's nothing like hearing the testimonies and seeing the hands raised (yes, I peek). But if I don't allow God to speak to me each week, change me, seeing God move in others will only last me so long.
>
> The danger is that it sneaks up on you. With a family to care for, a house to manage, and responsibilities at our church, it is easy to let the

urgent take the place of the important. Before you know it, you find yourself in a funk and burnt out. If I don't continually cultivate my own faith I will not make it in ministry. Awareness is definitely the first step. Action should follow. There aren't any cut-and-dried action steps. Mine would be different than yours. But I can start with a simple prayer, "Lord, I want to know you. Reveal yourself to me today. I will obey whatever you tell me."[1]

Make your faith your own. And get ready for a wild ride. It's a decision you'll never regret.

PARALYZED

Why would we ever allow someone else's relationship with Christ to define ours? Why would we ever choose *not* to be the person God created us to be? Unfortunately, many times the answers are fear and doubt. We're so terribly guilty of being afraid of messing up, not meeting an expectation, or disappointing someone that there are times we're frozen in fear. We allow fear to stop us from fully experiencing our roles, fully trusting, and fully exposing flaws.

Recently, I (Brandi) was battling some fear about a certain issue. Insecurity is an issue I've encountered before, and I'm sure it's something I'll face again. I was spending time at a restaurant with some women I love, women who are dear friends and who truly help shape me. I should have been enjoying the company and laughing my way through the evening, but instead my insecurity got the best of me. Women who loved me were sitting around the table sharing stories, laughter, and life. All my mind could focus on was that they had things more together than I did—that they were living up to their potential while I felt as if I was floundering. I wasn't even sure why they liked me, since I really didn't have much to offer. Insecurity grew from a small pebble in my shoe to a life-sized monster in the time it took our food to be delivered to the table. It caused me to doubt myself, doubt my capabilities, doubt my decisions, and I honestly wanted to hide out in a cave. I was *done*.

The next morning as I was flipping through my journal and going through some sermon notes from a few years back, something jumped out at me. It was one of those moments when my journal opened to the exact page I needed to read, and God gently reminded me: I am not plagued with self-doubt...instead, I doubt God.

We don't doubt ourselves. We doubt God's ability to use us. We doubt His ability to uniquely create us for the path He has laid out. He chose us for these positions. He carefully placed us as pastors' wives, ministry leaders, and influencers. Unfortunately, that fear and doubt often leave us paralyzed. And being paralyzed means you're wholly incapable of moving forward in God's design for you. Living life paralyzed by fear and doubt means you're going to miss out. The cost of missing out is greater than the cost of messing up.

But we don't want to miss out. Not as mothers, as wives, as friends, as Christ followers, and certainly not as pastors' wives or women in ministry. God has something so much better for us. When we realize that fear and doubt are paralyzing us, the good news is that we're the ones with the power to change. Isn't it nice to know you've got the power?

One of the first steps we two took to help define our personal callings was reevaluating our strengths. Since our current leading occupations were being stay-at-home-moms, we hadn't gotten around to evaluating our strengths outside of how fast we could wipe little noses or potty train to a defined level of success, so we were due a good evaluation. According to the *StrengthsFinder 2.0* test, a popular online assessment created to help people uncover their talents, Brandi's strengths are "Positivity, Consistency, Harmony, Communication, and Empathy." Lori's strengths are "Positivity, Belief, Developer, Communication, and Strategic." Our first response was: *Boooooooring!* (in our best eye-rolling ten-year-old whiny voices), but we've long gotten over that. Our strengths may not be the most fun or the flashiest, but they are ours. They are part of how God uniquely created us.

You, too, should discover your strengths. Take a test, ask a friend, spend some time in prayer, and become aware of your unique God-given strengths. Evaluation allows us to refocus and narrow in on what we should be doing, where we flourish, and how to have impact. It is an analysis of our commitments and of how we're spending our time. We were aware that to work in our personal callings, we needed to evaluate how God had gifted us. No doubt He created us each as a unique person, and a big part of finding how we serve best in ministry has to be developed around our unique gifts.

Knowing how God created you is as important as knowing how you best experience God.

This will come as a surprise, but we occasionally have rough mornings in the Wilhite and Wilson homes. There are mornings where spats break out, backpacks are forgotten, shoes are missing, and yells of "Don't touch me!" reverberate through our houses. We try to maintain calm exteriors, but sometimes you just can't handle one more little voice whining about the lunch in the Star Wars lunch box. We need to connect with God *stat*.

For me (Brandi), worship has always been my direct pathway to God. I pop in the earbuds and turn up the worship playlist. It takes just one song to connect with my heart and center myself back with Him. Stress and tension fade into the background, and I am allowed to "be still" and rest in His presence. Since Creation is a close second, a good run on a hiking trail with my worship playlist is awful close to heaven on earth!

Throw me (Lori) into a coffee shop with a few friends and a Bible study, and I am instantly encouraged and drawn closer to the Lord. My strong relational pathway allows God to use time spent in community to bolster my personal walk. When I am serving God to the best of my ability, my heart is full. Jumping in and helping people in need and being used by God to reach out to others connects me even more strongly to Him.

It's important to know your pathway to God. What draws you to Him with an intensity you can't define? What can align you to His presence when you feel distant from Him? Your pathway can attune you to hear His voice with a clarity that brings comfort.

THE MIMIC

Oftentimes, we don't seek out our personal calling because we're so wrapped up in looking at the gifts of those around us.

Brandi's youngest, Brewer, is a mimic. He came out of the womb trying to keep up with his brothers. He has learned so much about life by observing them and then following suit. He walked the earliest, has fully dressed himself since age two, and has been trying his darnedest the last few months to create a loose front tooth. Those attributes could point to a variety of things—his perseverance, his developed fine motor skills, and his birth order.

But Brewer's an impersonator. He recently received a new Bible in his kids' ministry class and was so proud to show it off to the family; he would hold it up and flip through the pages for everyone to see all the words. As soon as he walked in the front door with it, he grabbed a Sharpie and proceeded to ask every member of the family to sign his Bible. He wanted his brothers and amused parents to sign his new book the way his brothers had asked friends to sign their school yearbooks at the end of the year.

It's sweet watching him follow in his brothers' footsteps. But our desire is that he will develop the person he is uniquely created to be as well, that he will find his gifting and see his individuality.

So often in our own lives we're also mimics. If something works well for another pastor's wife, we decide to adjust our lives to match theirs. Observing another family functioning well makes us want to rearrange our parenting styles. Experiencing how someone else leads triggers us to take our cues from them instead of searching for our own direction—finding what God desires for us. We see success in another leader's ministry and change ours to match it. Before we know it, we can be living someone else's life and missing our own.

When we're tempted to mimic, we always come back to Galatians 6:5: *Each of you must take responsibility for doing the creative best you can with your own life.*[2] We're not saying we can't take helpful "pieces" from one another. Some of our greatest takeaways come from other leaders and parents. Many godly people around us have greatly influenced who we are as individuals and helped us develop into the people God created us to be. But be true to yourself. Be your own creative best, not someone else's creative best. Trust who God created you to be. Rest in knowing He's made you capable and unique. Don't just mimic your way through life. Instead, realize the truth in what our friend Lisa Hughes, a senior pastor's wife in Florida, says: "God has supernaturally scripted a customized plan with my name on it, and He has a supernaturally customized script for you. God has wired me, gifted me, and uniquely placed me in the ministry He has me in now. There is no other person He wants for this role other than me. And there is no other person He wants for your role other than you."[3]

Not long ago, I (Lori) was going through the mail when I came across a bulky cylinder from the local women's prison. When I opened the package, out poured a letter and five rolled canvases painted with lovely sunsets and tranquil beach scenes. Having only a little bit of oil paint and a little bit of unstretched canvas, a sweet woman had sent us all that she had to give. No money. No resources. No opportunity to volunteer. But the willingness to share what she had in the hope that God would use it for His kingdom.

Looking at those paintings, I was convicted.

I am not an amazing Bible teacher like Kay Warren and Beth Moore.

I am not an inspiring writer like Lysa TerKeurst.

I am not an incredible leader of women's ministry like Bobbi Houston from Hillsong Church.

And the list could go on.

A depressing number of years have been spent feeling as if we didn't measure up—feeling as if we were lacking, and holding back because of fear and insecurity. We don't know what your little bit of oil paint and canvas is in your life, ministry, and leadership. Do you hold it back or wonder in the corners of your mind if you are failing to measure up? Be reminded that God will put it to good use when you offer it up, in the way only you can, in the position in which God has placed you.

At the tender age of nine, our sweet friend Kimberly Scott, whose story we shared in the last chapter, absolutely adored her mom, who was also a pastor's wife. Kimberly respected, loved, and longed to emulate her mom. One day, she turned her eyes up at her momma and said, "I want to be just like you."

Her mom, with such grace and wisdom, replied, "Oh, honey, don't ever rob the Kingdom of God of who *you* were meant to be. Don't waste your time try-ing to be someone else. God has a unique purpose for your life, and *only you* can fulfill it."

How many of us now, at the ripe ages of twenty-six...thirty-eight...fifty-two...need to hear those words? We look at others, striving to lead like them, minister like them, serve like them, be like them. But all along God is whispering in our ears for us to be who He *created* us to be, who He *needs* us to be. Have you been robbing the Kingdom of God of who you were meant to be? Have you been trying to be someone you are not? Do you need to rest in the purpose only you can fulfill?

GUILT VS CONVICTION

Another area to consider when looking at your per-sonal calling is where your motivation comes from. One of the main things to weigh when making big decisions in leadership, especially when considering calendar issues, events to attend, and ministries to start or lead, is: Am I motivated out of guilt or conviction?

A few years ago, we noticed that most of our friends who were senior pastors' wives were leading and teach-ing in their women's ministries. The truth is, both of us felt downright guilty that we weren't doing more with ours. We started talking to lots of our friends, asking what they were doing with their women's ministries. We both thought, debated, and prayed. Honestly, we

didn't want to lead our women's ministries, but we
wrestled with guilt and tried to decide what we were
going to do. At one point or another, we asked each
other, "Are we slackers because we're not leading our
women's ministries?"

Luckily, we both realized we should never lead a
ministry out of guilt. Guilt is not from the Lord.
Now, conviction, that's an entirely different story.
Conviction is the work of the Holy Spirit. Conviction
is the right motivation to do something. It is crazy
to do something outside of the will and conviction of
God.

Realizing that truth allowed us to ask ourselves the
hard questions: Am I reacting to guilt because I feel
as if I'm not measuring up to my buddies, or am I
reacting out of conviction from the Holy Spirit? Ultimately, the answer was easy. We knew instantly it
wasn't conviction. We were both convicted to serve
God by ministering to pastors' wives and women in
leadership through Leading and Loving It. So we followed conviction.

Now, when wrestling with leadership decisions big
or small, we try to lay this question over the situation.
Does our motivation come from guilt or conviction?
God's goal is for us to flourish in ministry. And we'll
never flourish if we're leading and serving out of
guilt.

In his book *The Me I Want to Be*, John Ortberg addresses flourishing versus languishing in your spiritual walk. Flourishing is simply defined by asking yourself, "How am I blessing those around me?" Languishing also involves a straightforward question, "Am I growing more easily discouraged these days?" or "Am I growing more easily irritated these days?"[4]

These questions are so useful in our ministries and in figuring out if we're being the best "me." Are we serving with the correct intentions? Are we serving out of expectations? Are we growing more discouraged and tired as we serve? Are we spending more time being irritated with our circumstances? If you're answering yes to these questions, you're in a period of languishing. Honestly, we all go through periods of languishing, but we must make sure we don't get stuck there. They are moments we're embarrassed by. Moments we want to hide rather than discuss. Don't get comfortable languishing. Strive for flourishing. Strive for serving in a way that feeds you, keeps you excited about the work you're doing for Christ. You won't flourish if you're serving in someone else's footsteps. Flourishing will come in the ability to be completely you.

COMFORT VS GROWTH

Functioning in your personal calling means you're going to be forced to grow. However, sometimes we get so comfortable with leadership that we don't push ourselves toward growth and increasing our capacity. We've heard it said many times in many different situations: *Stop feeding what you want to die and starving what you want to live.*

That one sentence speaks volumes in so many areas of our lives. Over the years, we have developed horrible habits of investing in the things we *don't* want to grow in our lives while taking the quick way out with the qualities we'd like to develop. For instance:

It's easier to crash on the couch and blaze through one of our fiction books than it is to spend some quality time studying God's Word.

Grabbing a burger and fries is so much quicker and easier than preparing a healthy salad at home.

Curling up and watching a movie is effortless, while spending a disciplined hour at the gym has to be deliberate and can cause some discomfort to our rarely worked-out abs.

We can spend meaningless hours staring at Facebook status updates and Twitter feeds on our computer screens, while investing in friendships takes intentionality and energy.

The list could go on and on. It seems we, at times, develop a pattern of keeping unsatisfying, brief, and often damaging joys closest at hand while totally pushing away the great joy and growth that are achieved through struggle, pain, and quantity of time. The best encouragement on this comes from Jesus Himself, who reminds us it's all about the reward we will receive at the end of this earthly life. So when you don't feel like doing what you know is best for you, take heart and don't give in.

A GREAT WOMAN

Our friend Tiffany Cooper, a senior pastor's wife in Oklahoma, recently wrote an article defining "A Great Church."[5] We loved the post and almost instantly started adapting it to define a great woman in ministry.

God loves diversity. Look around; there is evidence of His creative diversity in all aspects of Creation. No two people or animals are alike. Our diversity is what makes life exciting. It's what keeps us on our toes and pushes us to be better. We are all originals to the core.

A great pastor's wife is...A great woman in ministry is...

> ...an introvert, an extrovert
> ...domestic, hates to cook
> ...serving on the front lines, working behind the scenes
> ...functioning in a traditional position, breaking the mold
> ...young, more mature

...serving in big churches, serving in small
  churches

...a morning person, a night owl

...a procrastinator, an overachiever

...a visionary, a cheerleader

...all about the details, loves the big picture

...patient, impatient

...organized, disorganized

...loves an audience, shies away from the spotlight

In the end, all pastors' wives and women in leadership should be women who proclaim the good news of
Jesus Christ and are driven to bring others to Him by
using their own unique gifts.

That, my friends, is what makes you a "famous
pastor's wife," a "famous woman in ministry." God
is not sorry He chose us. He's not sorry He chose
you. In fact, He's chosen each of us to do something of profound impact. We will not allow fear to
sideline us, to paralyze us and keep us from doing
what we've been chosen to do. But most important,
we are not on this journey alone. It's a path He
has prepared. You are a "famous pastor's wife" or a
"famous woman in ministry" because God *chose you!*
As His Word says in Galatians 1:15: *But even before
I was born, God chose me and called me by his marvelous
grace.*

As Lynne Hybels has written in her book *Nice Girls Don't Change the World*: "Never doubt that a community of thoughtful, committed women, filled with the power and love of God, using gifts they have identified and developed, and pursuing passions planted in them by God—never doubt that these women can change the world."[6]

CHAPTER 4

Marriage

I have been known to whine to my husband
that I have become a "ministry widow."

Confession

IN DECEMBER 1996 the air was crisp and cold: the kind
of air that makes your breath look thick and smoky.
With hair curled and sprayed, makeup painstakingly
applied, and beaded ivory dresses in tow, we each
made our way to beautifully decorated churches. Exactly two weeks apart, Jud and Lori married in West
Texas and Pete and Brandi married in small-town
Kentucky. Gaudy brass candelabras and poinsettias
filled the front of the sanctuaries, hiding the wonders
of puke-green and wine-colored carpets. Those were
the days we married our husbands. They were also the
days we became pastors' wives.

At the ages of twenty-one and twenty-two, we had
very limited knowledge of marriage and ministry. Our

romantic notions had been shaped by Victorian-era novels and Hollywood chick flicks. We thought our marriages and our lives in ministry would be wonderful and easy. How could they not be? We had married incredible men; what difficulty could possibly follow? We had no idea that the people in our churches would make assumptions about our marriages and home lives based on a few comical sermon illustrations. You don't have to be married long before you realize marriage is hard work. Anytime two sinners are united as one, there are bound to be a few bumps in the road.

Pete became aware of a new "friend" he would soon grow to despise—my (Brandi's) yellow shower cap. I will never forget the look on Pete's face the first time I stepped out of the shower wearing that yellow shower cap. His new bride, the woman he expected to—using his own words—"look hot twenty-four/seven," was wearing something he thought only ladies over the age of seventy-five should put on. He stood speechless as I tried to explain, "I don't like to wash my hair every day," and "I've had this shower cap since high school, I can't part with it now." I've since been presented with a red sequined shower cap, but it really doesn't make a difference; every time I step out of the shower wearing that cap we both start to giggle.

Jud, on the other hand, discovered a few new "friends" of his own. A few days before we (Lori and Jud) got married, Jud said, "I'm just ready to have your stuff around my stuff." Little did he know that my stuff would literally fill our tiny bathroom. He was suddenly surrounded by dainty floral-smelling jars, hair dryer and curling iron cords dangling over the sink, and five different hair products he'd never heard of before. I'm sure that weeks into our marriage he was frantically trying to figure out a way to get his tiny bag of toiletries its own space. My stuff wasn't just *around*; it had completely taken over!

Marriages take work and intentionality. People rarely drift into happy, healthy marriages; we must make purposeful efforts toward that end. Add in ministry and a few extra little bodies crawling and running around the house, and you seriously have your work cut out for you. But as Jud Wilhite often says, "The best thing you can do for your family is have a healthy, thriving marriage. The best thing you can do for your church family is have a healthy, thriving marriage." Because we are leaders, our marriages affect not only us as individual couples, but also our children, our families, and yes, our congregations as well.

So let's take a look at some ways to maintain our marriages while navigating our lives in leadership.

TALK. TALK. TALK.
Communication, as we all know, is vital in our relationships. We need time to download the day, share the highs and lows of work, home, and school. But there

is a temptation for some of us, for myriad reasons, to hold back—to not communicate with our husbands about our feelings or struggles.

A few years ago I (Lori) hit a major speed bump in the road of our marriage. It seemed as though there was an unending list of things Jud needed to do. He worked hard, long hours. And to put it bluntly, I felt abandoned. I had a two-year-old and a newborn at home. I spent my days with diapers, dolls, and Dora the Explorer. For close to a year, I felt as if I rarely saw my husband. I didn't really feel that I was sharing him with the church; it felt more as if they had taken him hostage and I was going to be hard pressed to get him back.

The record that played in the back of my mind stated over and over that if Jud was called by God to this work, then I was going to have to suck it up and take one for the team. So I did. I took a deep breath, put my head down, and continued to function in my everyday life as a stay-at-home mom. But over that year, bitterness took root, and I was silent about what was going on in my heart and life.

Our marriage-saving moment arrived as that year came to a close. I was talking on the phone to a friend late one night and confessed to her that I felt much like a single mom. As God would have it, Jud walked by at just the right moment. He was upset to learn that I felt so alone and abandoned. He was shocked; he'd had no idea I felt that way! We sat down, and for the first time, I laid out all that I had been feeling. Shockingly, he hadn't been able to read my mind. Can you imagine?

No more silence. No more taking one for the team. It was time to address our emotional, spiritual, and relational health. We needed to do the hard work to get our marriage back to a healthy place. I'm so glad that Jud was accidentally eavesdropping that day! I don't know how long I would have let it go before saying something.

We (Lori and Brandi) don't know what is blocking you from sharing the struggles and conflicts going on in your heart and life, but please don't cover them in silence any longer. Have the hard conversations so you can begin moving forward as a couple, on the same team, toward a healthier marriage.

In every marriage there is always one person who is a little more intuitively dialed into the relational dynamics. If that's you, one thing that can really help communication in marriage is laying out where your relationship is in black-and-white. Let your husband know exactly where your marriage is on a scale of 1 to 10. When you give your score, grading on a curve is not allowed. If you're just going to round up a few numbers to make your husband feel good, it won't work. You must be willing to give an honest number, and he must be willing to hear the number without defensiveness. Now, what do you do with that number?

Check out this advice from one of Brandi's girl-friends: "When I look at improving our marriage, instead of shooting for a solid ten, I try to focus on one notch at a time. For instance, let's say my marriage is at a six right now; I'm only looking at moving it to a seven. Shooting for ten all the time gets exhausting. I've learned to celebrate the small successes."

Such a simple concept, but it's so much easier to look at loving our husbands better one small step at a time. For instance, Pete was getting ready to go out of town and was loading up his suitcase. He kindly asked if I (Brandi) could iron the collar of a shirt he was packing. I did it, but I'll be honest and say I didn't do it with a cheerful heart. I might have even added in a few "You know I hate ironing" and "Won't there be an iron in your hotel?" comments. Looking back, I see that I turned a simple sixty-second chore into a "situation." He was already feeling the pressure of a busy week and a hectic travel schedule; he didn't need to hear his wife's negative commentary or her view on ironing. Loving him better at that moment simply meant being his helpmate with a giving spirit.

THE BEST OFFENSE IS A GOOD DEFENSE

Lori spent many a Friday night under the lights of Texas high school football stadiums, and Brandi's blood runs the blue of the Tennessee Titans. The two of us have a serious love for football, which is the best sport. Ever. As any football great would acknowledge, the best offense is a good defense. Yes, it surely is. Some things just transcend football.

If our marriages are going to function at their healthiest (and we mean the marriages of all us ladies, not just Lori's and Brandi's), we need to make sure to have a great defensive strategy. This isn't because we don't trust our husbands, or because we can't control ourselves. We need a good defense because not a single one of us is above temptation. And the enemy would love to destroy the marriages of those in leadership because the fallout of those broken marriages is tremendous.

As Oswald Chambers has pointed out in *My Utmost for His Highest:* "An unguarded strength is actually a double weakness."[1] No matter how strong our marriages may be, if we turn a blind eye to the things that threaten them, we are leaving our relationships unguarded and weak. Statistics on pastors and other church leaders who have had extramarital affairs vary widely, but it's likely we all know at least one friend or colleague who has been through that heartbreak—maybe you have walked through that painful valley in your own marriage.

While each couple should come up with its own defense strategy, here are a few of the things we do to
guard our marriages.

- Jud and Lori don't meet with anyone of the op-
  posite sex alone, not for lunch, not for counseling,
  not at all.
- Pete and Brandi practice an "open ask" policy.
  They each know that at any time, they have the
  opportunity to ask about a situation that needs
  clarification or a circumstance that makes them uncomfortable.
- As much as possible, Pete and Jud don't travel
  alone. If they do, they try to stay with friends
  once they reach their destination. It can't always be
  done, but they try the best they can.
- Date times are a priority. Whether it is Taco Bell
  picnics in front of the TV when little ones are
  asleep or breakfast alone after dropping bigger
  kids off at school, time alone connecting, laughing,
  and having fun together is needed.
- Share your passwords. Give your spouse complete
  access to your online world—Facebook, Twitter,
  and e-mail. According to a recent article, "More
  than a third of divorce filings last year contained
  the word Facebook....And over 80% of U.S. divorce attorneys say they've seen a rise in the number of cases using social networking."[2] Complete

transparency with our spouses in our online lives is a great defense strategy.

IT'S GOD'S JOB

Have you ever wondered what it's like to be married to you? What is it like to be on the receiving end of the love and respect (or lack thereof) you show others? Eek. Those are powerful and convicting questions that each of us should wrestle with on a regular basis. While we might love to change a few things about our spouses to make married life a bit easier, that just isn't possible. We can't control or change our husbands, and neither can you. As Billy Graham's wife, Ruth, has so eloquently stated, "It is God's job to change Billy. It is my job to love him."[3] It isn't Brandi's job to change Pete, but to love him. It isn't Lori's job to change Jud, but to love him. And it isn't your job to change your spouse. Your job is to love him.

Some of you struggle, sitting under the teaching of your husband. You wrestle with past hurts or arguments, and it is difficult to receive the Word from him. Some of you are heartbroken about the sin issues going on in your husband's life. You are frustrated because you see two different men during the week, one at the church and another at home. Some of you are jealous because your husband is quick to pray with a stranger in the hall but hasn't prayed with you in months.

While God is doing the continued redemptive work in the lives of our husbands, it's our job to lift our guys up to the Lord in prayer. It is probably the single most powerful thing we can do in our marriages. Consider this, from the Leading and Loving It prayer challenge written by our friend Natalie Witcher, a family pastor's wife:

Pray for his relationship with Jesus. Above all things, the relationship our husbands have with Jesus is the most important. It's most important above the church, above family, and above us. When they are operating out of the relationship with Christ and the power of His Spirit, everything else starts to follow suit. Take the next few moments to pray this prayer.

"Jesus, You are over all. You are the mighty Savior of all who would call on Your name, and then You are the powerful Sender of those who say, "Yes!" My husband has said yes. So, I pray that he and You are so close and so entwined that my husband can't help but walk by Your Spirit. I pray that he is rooted and established in love. I pray that You are the author and perfector of his faith. I pray that he casts all his cares on You and unloads with all thanksgiving. I pray You are his most trusted confidant, most valiant leader, and closest friend. Jesus, be his everything. In Your powerful name I ask."

Pray for his relationship with you. While Christ is

his #1, you need to be his #2. Sometimes we can feel like the church is second, but nagging him about it won't help. What we must do out of love is pray for our relationships with our husbands. Some of you probably have an incredible relationship with your man, others of you might really be hurting. Whatever your situation with your husband, talking to Jesus about it is the best way to enhance it, change it, purify it, and love it.

"Jesus, married life is wild, fun, hard, and purposeful. I want to lift my husband to You and thank You for putting us together. It's so important to me that he and I have a strong and loving relationship. Help us be to one another what You want us to be: loving and respectful. I know that when I honor him and he loves me, there is no stopping us! I pray that we both are humbled to You in order to love one another more deeply and more powerfully. Thank You for what You are doing in our marriage and what You will do in the future. I leave us to You. In Your sweet name, Jesus."

Pray for his relationship with your family. Our children are such a beautiful extension of who we are. We can even see our husbands' eyes and lips and nose in their faces. They reflect him. Jesus reflected the very glory of God. Let's pray our husbands lead our families in such a way that their children reflect their honor, grace, mercy, leadership, and a host of other Christlike characteristics.

"God, my family is my heartbeat on the outside of my body! I want them to know You more than anything. I pray that through what my husband does, they will see a life committed to the One who died for them. I pray that through what my husband says, they will know what tender grace is and that gracious discipline is from You. I pray that through what my husband speaks, they will understand servant-leadership, wisdom, vision, and knowledge. I pray that through how my husband laughs, they will know the joy of Christ. And I pray that through how my husband loves, our family will know the love of You, Father. Thank You for this family. We offer ourselves to You, in the name of Jesus."

Pray for his leadership. This is probably the area we pray for the most. Leading people is no small task. Leading our families isn't one, either. Since it's such a massive part of what our husbands do, let's not fail to pray for them again in this area.

"God, leadership is built in us. At some level, we are all leaders. You created us to rule and lead and show the way to others. Jesus mandated that we go into the world and make disciples, so my husband needs an unleashing in the area of leadership. I pray that he is in tune with Your gentle, yet powerful Spirit, who reminds us of all Jesus said. I pray that he surrounds himself with others who sharpen his leadership skills and stretch him to become a greater man, full of in-

tegrity and honor as he leads those You have given
him. Give him strength, wisdom, vision, and the grace
to do it all. Thank You for leading him as he leads others. I ask our Leader, Jesus, in Your name to do all
this."

Pray for his protection. You don't have to live long
as a Christ follower to know our enemy isn't playing
around when it comes to trying to trick, trap, or destroy us. What your husband is doing not only perks
up the ears of Satan, but also riles up his anger. When
Jesus said that Satan came to kill, steal, and destroy,
that meant us; that meant your man. Fight for him in
prayer.

"Great and powerful Jesus! We've tasted the fruit
of sin and know the sweetness in our mouths and the
punch of bitterness in our soul. We've chosen the path
of falling for the lies of the enemy before, and it is no
way to go. I know that in the position my husband is in,
he is a target. He's a target of the enemy who will do
whatever he can to see my husband come to ruin. So
I pray boldly to You in the power of Your Spirit that
You protect him with the mighty name of Jesus. You
have overcome the world and are greater than he who
is in it, and I pray that my husband walks in that every
day. I pray for accountability and friendships that will
pray for him as well. He has a job to do and no time
to be dealing with Satan. Protect him by the mighty
power of Your name, Jesus!"[4]

OUR JOB

Having left the life-changing work of our husbands to God, we can now concentrate on the one person in our marriages we can control: ourselves. How can we best perform our jobs of loving our husbands well? Let's take a look at a very familiar passage for married couples, Ephesians 5:33. Paul writes that *each man must love his wife as he loves himself, and the wife must respect her husband.* In order to follow through on our jobs, we get our best Aretha Franklin on and show some R-E-S-P-E-C-T.

Respect is a huge need in the lives of our husbands. In a recent poll, 400 men were asked this question: "If you had to choose between being alone and unloved for the rest of your life or being disrespected by everyone, which would you choose?" A mind boggling seventy-five percent of the men said they would choose to be alone and unloved for the rest of their lives rather than be disrespected by everyone.[5] What?! No way. Most women would never choose to be alone and unloved. Right, ladies?

We (Lori and Brandi) have spent most of our marriages trying to make sure our husbands know how much we love them. However, not much effort, energy, or time had been spent trying to make sure they knew how much we respected them. If respect was the primary need in their lives, we weren't meeting that need. Significant changes had to be made in our communication to make sure they knew how much they were respected.

Stay away from complaining. One of the fastest ways for us to communicate disrespect to the men in our lives is nagging. In her great book *What's It Like to Be Married to Me?*, Linda Dillow shares the 21-Day No-Complaint Challenge.[6] Here's the deal. Find yourself an incredibly cute, trendy bracelet that easily slips on and off. Every time—yes, every single time—a complaint, gripe, or bit of grouchiness comes out of your mouth, move your bracelet to the other arm. Pretty simple, right?

When we first launched into this challenge, we thought it was going to be a piece of cake. No problem. We are pretty positive gals, natural encouragers. Sure, we've read that we are to *do everything without complaining and arguing*, as Paul says in Philippians 2:14. Now, we are no theologians, but our understanding is that *everything* actually means *everything*. So with that in mind, half an hour hadn't passed before those bracelets made the first of many journeys to the other wrist. Over the next three weeks, quite a few benefits emerged from the No-Complaint Challenge. First, as we became aware of each complaint, whine, or criticism coming out of our mouths, it was quite obvious how many unimportant things drove us to gripe. The majority of the time, our complaining would have no effect on the object of our complaint. The weather doesn't care if we'd rather not have our hair crazy wind-blown as we head into church. Our clocks don't move more slowly even if our to-do list is growing longer than what can be accomplished in a twenty-four-hour period. The only people being affected by the majority of our complaints were us.

Secondly, as we started to take complaints captive before they exited our mouths, our thought lives started to change as well. There was an intentional re-focus of our thoughts onto better things. We forcibly had to *Fix [our] thoughts on what is true, and honorable, and right, and pure, and lovely, and admirable. Think about things that are excellent and worthy of praise*, as Philippians 4:8 says. Thirdly, as gratitude grew instead of grouch-iness, our homes became even more pleasant places. It's not surprising that when we ceased voicing the nagging and complaining to our husbands, their atti-tudes and demeanors were positively affected. Maybe it was just our perception that changed, but everyone seemed happier and more peaceful. It was a beautiful thing.

These were the benefits from just three small, im-perfect weeks of keeping the No-Complaint Challenge at the front of our minds. Can you imagine the dif-ference it could make in your marriage if done for the long haul? Linda Dillow says the average person needs "four to eight months to string together twenty-one gripe-free days."[7] Whoa. That's lots of bracelet moving, but what an incredible difference not complaining could make in our marriages, families, and friendships!

Honor your husband. Once the complaints and criticisms are taken captive, we have many opportunities to instead find ways to honor our husbands. Instead of sitting with a friend or your mom over coffee complaining about your husband, take a few minutes to talk about the things you are thankful for about him. Instead of nagging your guy about the unaccomplished honey-do list, tell him what he does that you are grateful for; list his strengths and gifts. Let him know exactly what you respect about him. Then watch him transform before your eyes. Taking time and being intentional about honoring our husbands will not only mean the world to them, but it will also do a great work in our own hearts and spirits as we seek to focus our thoughts on those positives laid out in Philippians 4:8. It will move our hearts from grumpiness to gratitude.

Be your husband's biggest cheerleader. He has plenty of voices and angry e-mails pointing out his weak spots and mistakes. It's our job to be the loudest voice of encouragement in his life. Try some of these practical ways of encouraging your husband, tweeted to us by ladies in the Leading and Loving It community:

"I don't just tell him his sermon was great; I tell
   him exactly what God spoke to my heart
   through the message."

"I listen to the thought process of his message
   and give him honest feedback. He usually
   wows me!"

"I always smile and give a big kiss before he
   leaves for church, with an 'I love you.'"

"I watch and listen in to his work (media) when
   I can. I (mostly) make his lunch."

"I send him text messages. Some sweet, flirty,
   often simple phrase or prayer."

"I tell him I believe in him."

"I pursue him physically. ;)"

"I will put a card in his desk for him to find."

"His love language is words of affirmation. I
   think it but forget to say it. If I think it, I
   should say it."

"Brag about him to others when he's in close
   proximity! Women have better peripheral vision so it's easy to gauge this!"

"I let him know that I trust his decisions for our
   church and our family."

As we commit to respecting, honoring, and loving
our husbands well, there is still one voice that matters
most. Want to hear one of my (Brandi's) deepest, darkest marriage secrets? We repeatedly fight over direc-

tions. I'm talking moments of intense fellowship, if ya know what I mean. It's happened for years. It's not his fault. It's not my fault. It's just how we function when we're traveling together. And by traveling together, I mean sometimes we're just going across town, and we still might argue about how to get there.

Around one of our recent wedding anniversaries, I realized I was never going to be able to "fix" our directional differences. We've rationally discussed these directional issues many times in the past, and he believes I should be his navigator. But guess what? I don't like being his navigator.

So I decided to take action with his anniversary gift. When he arrived home from work that afternoon, there was a wrapped gift with a note that said:

I love being your partner in life, but I lovingly resign as your navigator. For our anniversary I'm giving you another woman. Say hello to Eleanor.

Yes, for our anniversary I gave my husband another woman—Eleanor, the GPS navigating system. Eleanor went to work immediately, accompanying us on our date later that evening, and we both fell in love with her. Not only did we arrive at our destination without argument, we actually arrived with smiles. And the best part of it all, Eleanor has an English accent, and we all know everything sounds better with an accent.

That third voice in our car made all the difference on the way to dinner that night. Our marriages must also have a third voice guiding us. It is essential in our marriage relationships to allow God's voice and His word to guide us as we walk through life as one flesh. It's His voice that will provide respect, guidance, affirmation, and encouragement. It's His voice that will pull you together in difficult seasons. It's His voice that will counsel you as you lead in your churches. It's His voice that will guide you to a healthy, thriving marriage, affecting not only your families, but your churches as well.

CHAPTER 5

Raising Kids

I hate knowing that people will judge my kids
according to their parents' profession (as they
get older).

Confession

I dread having children because I don't want
the advice of the church members, and I don't
want to be judged for the choices I will make
when raising them.

Confession

AS SHE WALKED the fluorescent-lit aisles of the video
store, fifteen-year-old Tiffany's biggest concern that
Friday night in 1994 was whether to rent the feel-
good *Forrest Gump* or the tear-jerking *Schindler's List*.
Suddenly she was cornered by her piano teacher, who
spewed forth a warning that Tiffany's dad was a false
teacher leading her down a dangerous path. Knowing
the claim was untrue didn't ease the extreme hurt Tiffany felt. The wind had been completely knocked out

of her. How was she supposed to respond? Like every good girl who wants to do the right thing, she listened while her heart painfully shattered into pieces. She felt lost as she grappled for something to say in response. Tiffany's dad, the greatest man she knew, was being verbally torn to shreds right in front of her face. Unfortunately, that was only the first of many painful moments she went through, growing up as the pastor's kid. Ministry was a blessing, but sometimes it sure felt like a curse.

Living every day in the public eye was incredibly challenging. People examined her every word and scrutinized every action. She was overwhelmed. At fifteen, Tiffany realized that she would never measure up to the perfection people expected and began to live a false life. She stuffed her struggles behind a big, fake smile and put up a wall to prevent people from seeing her imperfections. Soon she began to crumble on the inside and started rebelling in secret so she wouldn't bring embarrassment to her parents or the church.

Tiffany was consumed by what people thought of her, by her attempts to fit the perfect image. Although her parents never put one unhealthy expectation on her, she began to suffocate under the pressure of others' unspoken expectations. She felt as if she were throwing a dart in the air in hopes that it would land on the target. She wasn't exactly sure what she was supposed to be like, but she was going to attempt to hit the bull's-eye. Instead of hitting the mark, Tiffany completely lost focus. Her grades declined, she lost her ambition, and her confidence dwindled.

Tiffany went from being a motivated honor roll student her freshman and sophomore years to being a girl more obsessed with what she looked like and the perfect image she could portray in her junior and senior years. Guys poured attention on her, and she cared more about what they thought than what she knew was best for her. The attention she received distracted her from what really mattered.

During her junior year, she got caught shoplifting beauty products and gifts she wanted to give her friends for Christmas. Tiffany didn't want to burden her parents with things she felt she needed, so she just stole them. She had slowly gotten so far off track that she found herself doing things she'd never thought she would do. She felt lost and alone in a world where everyone expected her to have it together.

Between the two of us, we have five children: Lori with her raven-haired, dark-eyed, freckled boy-and-girl pair, and Brandi with her three blond-haired, blue-eyed, testosterone-filled stairstep little boys. We, along with our pastor husbands, are raising five children of God. Notice, even though we are married to pastors we choose not to use the term *pastors' kids* when describing our children. The initials *PK* have always made us cringe and seem to come with a set of expectations that other kids don't face. Why? Why, because their father is called by God to lead the church, do people expect them to behave differently? Why are some of these kids criticized more harshly when they make mistakes? Why do congregations feel they have the right to speak about the pastor's parenting techniques? It is baffling. There is a spotlight on ministry families; our kids face pressures that nonministry families don't face.

Even in the early years of parenting, when our children would display typical toddler misbehavior, someone would jokingly throw out the old "Already making trouble like a typical PK." We are pretty sure our nails extended a few inches, and we came incredibly close to clawing their eyes out. Our initial internal response was always defensive. Our response may not have been verbal, but on the inside our stomachs were churning at that simple, often innocent statement. Then our friend Jessica Cornelius, a senior pastor's wife in Corpus Christi, shared with us her response during similar situations. When someone addressed her kid as a PK, she (in her sweetest Texas accent) reminded the culprit, "They're just regular kids being raised by Christian parents." *Regular kids being raised by Christian parents.* Now, that is an expression to embrace and is much kinder than screaming *"Back off, lady!"* to an innocent bystander who might have just made a ridiculous statement.

Each of us will have our high and low moments as parents—our bright spots and not-so-bright spots. That's part of being a mom. A while ago, I (Lori) was heading home after a family dinner. We pulled up at a stoplight in front of a typical Vegas billboard. Splayed out on the billboard were the naked backs of six women with the words THE HITS ARE BACK covering their bottoms, because of course you need that kind of image to advertise your Classic Rock radio station. Suddenly I heard the sweet, innocent voice of my precious seven-year-old-son ring out from the backseat of our minivan: "Emma, which one of those naked girls is your favorite? Mine is the one with the brown hair."

Oh. My. Gosh.

In a moment of what can only be defined as sheer parenting brilliance, I whipped my head around and said, "Ethan, we do not have favorite naked girls!" Apparently naked girls are fine, just not favorites. Ugh. Not a shining moment for me as a mom. But don't worry, I've gotten to redeem myself with many more conversations about such things since then. Opportunity abounds.

Our kids will have those ups and downs as well. They make mistakes and dumb choices. They, like us, are sinners on the faith journey trying to live more like

Christ. We are just Christian parents guiding our children to the best of our ability. It has nothing to do with our jobs, our roles, or our churches. It has everything to do with Jesus, and we can feel free to make that clear to others as well as our children.

WE'RE NOT PARENTING ALONE

A few years back, former First Lady Hillary Rodham Clinton published a book entitled *It Takes a Village*. Regardless of your political beliefs, it's undeniable that the phrase *it takes a village* was immediately adopted into our language, popping up frequently when people discussed parenting. For instance, a girlfriend takes your child to baseball practice, and you shoot her a thank-you text that includes *It takes a village*. Because, let's be honest, parenting is hard, and life is busy. Sometimes when the heat of the spotlight is shining on our lives as leaders, we look at our children and see the spotlight shining even more brightly on them. Even though we might have used the *it takes a village* phrase, we suddenly feel very alone. The weight of raising Godly children in the spotlight feels like an enormous burden and is isolating for us as parents.

Recently Cross Point Church decided to partner with a local ministry, Lighthouse Ministries, to add some volunteers to the church's parking team. Lighthouse is a halfway house for men transitioning from being in prison to living back out in the world. They were amazing volunteers: dependable, friendly, and always sitting attentively through our morning services.

Not long after they started serving regularly, my (Brandi's) boys started asking questions, wondering who the new guys were who helped park cars. I briefly explained what Lighthouse was and how these guys were helping out, but let's be honest, my kids heard the word *jail* and could think of nothing else.

My boys always said hello to the parking team, but the whole *been in jail* definition left them a little leery. One morning on the way to church, I really spent some time talking to Jett, our oldest, about the guys who volunteer, and why at Cross Point we believe "Nobody's Perfect, Everyone's Welcome, and Anything's Possible." At the time, I thought I was teaching a life lesson to Jett; little did I know that that very Sunday I'd be reminded of an important lesson myself.

I sat in the service worshipping that morning as person after person was baptized. I noticed one Lighthouse gentleman who guides parking in the lot we use each week (the one my boys were most familiar with) walking forward for baptism. At that very moment I felt God say, "Brandi, this isn't a lesson just for Jett, but a lesson for you as well."

Our family is like yours, and church is a huge part of our lives. Yet sometimes I take for granted the way God works and the mystery that comes along with believing in Christ. The lesson on grace and second chances wasn't just for Jett; it was for me, too. It was a lesson in "you're not parenting alone." A lesson reminding me that the God of the universe knows the small conversation I'm having with my children on the way to church. Imagine my joy when on the way home that day I got to share with Jett that "jail guy" (as he's affectionately referred to) will spend eternity with us in heaven. It was a lesson I couldn't have created if I'd tried.

As Christians, not just ministry families, we are not parenting alone. God is watching over your children. He loves them more than you could ask or imagine. He hasn't given us the responsibility of raising pastors' kids, He's gifted us with the responsibility of raising children who grow up with a heart for Him. Children who know they are unconditionally loved by Him. Children who run to Him in times of trouble. Children who seek guidance from the wisest Counselor of all. We aren't raising PKs; we're raising kids for Christ. As isolated as we might feel at times, we aren't raising them alone.

Ministry kids aren't superhuman. They are regular kids who develop and grow at their own pace. What is our role in helping them as they juggle life in the spotlight? What advice can we give our kids on how to maneuver through the pressures they face?

*   *   *

Remind them they are His first. Over the years we've heard so many wise Christian parents tell us that the main thing they repeat to their children over and over again is "Remember Whose you are." Remember Whose you are when you're out with your friends. Remember Whose you are when you're at a football game. Remember Whose you are as you're tutoring that fellow student. Remember Whose you are as you head to college and live on your own. When that phrase is spoken, it isn't just about being a Wilson or a Wilhite. It's about being a child of God first—knowing Who you are called to serve in everything you do, knowing Whom to obey.

In order for our kids to "remember Whose they are," it's essential to teach them the unconditional love of Christ. Teaching our children that God loves them unconditionally needs to be the foundation on which they live their lives. We are the ones who set that foundation. They need to know that our God is the God of second chances. It's a message that is taught to our congregations and the people serving in our nonprofits, but is it a message we're teaching our children?

Our children will make mistakes, and in the midst of the turmoil of those mistakes, we must make sure they know to run toward Him, not away from Him. Nothing can ever separate them from His love. We must make sure they receive the grace we give everyone else. And ultimately, it is you and I who will be demonstrating His great love in their lives. Let's make sure our children see the friendship of God first played out in our homes. The better our children know Him, the clearer they'll be able to see His vision for their lives.

Have healthy expectations. We've written a whole chapter on expectations we have for ourselves, as well as expectations others have for us. Unfortunately, those expectations often trickle down to our children. That's usually where those terrible initials *PK* come into practice. Make sure as parents that the expectations you have for your children are based on where they are developmentally and on what Scripture says, not on the fact that they're PKs. Be an advocate for your children. They need to know without a shadow of a doubt that you're their biggest cheerleader both in the church and outside the church.

Not only is Holly Furtick a senior pastor's wife, she was also a pastor's kid. We really respect her advice on how her parents defined healthy expectations for Holly and her two sisters. She says:

"When you set rules for your children be sure those rules or standards are because you are Christ followers, not due to the expectations of the church. For instance, if your family chooses not to trick-or-treat make sure it's because it's not right for your family, not because the church wouldn't like it. If you enforce a dress code make sure the dress code is created out of what you feel is inappropriate everywhere, not just for church. Don't force your children to do something because of other people's expectations. You know them best!"[1]

We love the way our Leading and Loving It team member Tiffany Cooper and her husband, Herbert, have actually written out expectations for their children:

Our family is committed to God. We desire for you to grow in your relationship with God.

Our family is committed to each other. Family is our first ministry; your needs come before the church.

Our family is committed to church. You will attend faithfully and serve faithfully.

Everybody has an opinion. Kindly disregard opinions that don't line up with God's Word and our expectations of you.

Follow your heart. Do what you feel God has gifted you to do, not what others want you to do.

Always, under any circumstance, come to us about your struggles. We are a safe place for you to discuss your issues, good or bad.[2]

Having their expectations clearly laid out helps them keep their focus as they parent. It helps give their kids a reminder of what the guidelines are for their family.

Protect them. Our littlest guys, Brewer and Ethan, are introverts. They have big personalities once you get to know them, but it takes some work to get them out of their shells. Needless to say, getting them to feel comfortable at church has taken some work. Even as an infant Brewer would turn his face from someone leaning over his infant carrier to acknowledge him. Ethan would hide behind Mommy's leg and stay silent when crowds of people were trying to talk to him. As the boys got a little older, they would cling to us as soon as we got out of our cars and started toward the church. All the attention overwhelmed them. A very wise pediatrician, when asked about the shyness, reminded Brandi of something she should have known herself: her job was to protect Brewer. Lori's job was to protect Ethan. They might not love the attention their older siblings had gotten used to, and that was okay. Our job was to let them know they were fine, not to force them to talk, not even to force eye contact, but to allow them to be comfortable in that atmosphere because they knew we were their advocates.

Now, it should probably be clarified, we don't allow our shy guys to be rude. Let's be honest, none of us would want hundreds of strangers talking to us suddenly. It's our belief that as moms, we are the ones who know their personalities best, that protecting our children by allowing them to be the little introverts God created actually allows them to flourish and be comfortable with who they are. They are both taught manners, but sometimes those lessons are best taught in small groups of adults they're more comfortable with rather than in an audience full of strangers.

Protecting them doesn't end as they move through the elementary years. It continues as they grow and move into the teenage years. Our kids need to be clear that the expectations they are to respect are first those of God and then those of their parents. Being at home with their family should feel like being in a safe place. You are your children's greatest advocate; no other human will love them and protect them the way you can. Ensure that they know that their job as your children isn't to please the people of the church, but to please their Savior.

Accentuate the positive. Both of us love what we get to do and that God called our families to serve Him in the local church. But are there times when we don't love ministry? Times when we feel we're struggling more than celebrating? Seasons when we aren't pumped to go to church? Sure. During those times, we realize our children are following our lead, and we have to do our best at choosing to still love it. Our attitudes are contagious to our children. We can't let our frustration and weariness affect our children's attitude toward the church.

One recommended practice is to accentuate the positive. Even when finding the positive is work, we still choose to let our kids see the good with simple phrases like:

We are so blessed to have people who love our
    family so much.
Isn't it cool we get to see people come to Christ
    in our church?
Can you believe we get to serve God this way?
Isn't it fun we get to do this?

Speaking negatively about the Bride of Christ is avoided at all costs in front of our children, even if it means biting our tongues until they bleed. When we were beautiful brides dressed in our dream wedding gowns, imagine how our husbands would have reacted if they'd heard someone speak negatively about us. It would have been crushing to see something so beautiful degraded. It is important to have healthy discussions with our children about church, teaching them how to deal with difficult situations. We don't sugarcoat our way through life, but we are also vividly aware of the way we speak about the church we've been called to serve. Positives should always overshadow negatives. Living with the resurrected power of Jesus is something our children get to witness firsthand. For a parent, there are few blessings that are greater than that truth.

Be a thermostat. We've often heard: "Be the thermostat for your home, not the thermometer." Being visual gals, that metaphor is very clear to us. You're either one or the other. A thermostat *sets* the temperature, while the thermometer *reads* the temperature. A thermostat causes change; a thermometer is reactive. Look into the metaphor even deeper, and you'll realize we have the power to set the temperature of our homes.

Think your kids need an attitude adjustment? Then set the temp; model that attitude. Want them to develop a servant's heart? Set the temp; model a heart that loves others well. Trying to teach siblings to get along? Set the temp; show them healthy communication with your spouse.

Being an effective thermostat doesn't mean being strict, pushy, and loud. It has everything to do with your attitude. We influence a lot of environments on a daily basis; we need to make sure we're being thermostats that allow for growth and positive responses.

Serve with joy. One of the greatest impacts ministry can have on our kids is seeing the influence the church has outside their family unit. Often our children just view ministry or church as the position their family is connected to. They identify our churches through their fathers. When they think of their church, they think of their dad onstage teaching. We love the pride our children feel when they see their dads represent, but we also love it when they see their churches make a positive impression in their community and around the globe. The clearest way for our children to see that impact is through serving.

Recently I (Brandi) got the opportunity to do something with my two older boys I've dreamed about—take them on their first mission trip. We traveled with about eighty other Cross Pointers in a caravan of buses aimed for Wheelwright, a community nestled in the Appalachian Mountains of eastern Kentucky. The best way I can describe it is to say it's a forgotten community. Drugs and suicide are the two most popular pastimes. In this community of less than a thousand, they average two to four suicides a month. It's a place of true despair, and it's only a few hours from our home.

Cross Point has partnered with the Wheelwright community for about six years and visits at least three times each year. Strong relationships and deep trust have been formed. This visit with my boys was to deliver Christmas gifts to 187 children, as well as food and cleaning supplies for 90 families. We also hosted a Christmas party for families, playing games, making crafts, having family photos taken, giving haircuts, and enjoying hot meals.

The trip was one of intention for me. I wanted my children to experience the joy of serving others through missions, and I also wanted them to see their church in action. I wanted them to see the impact the church makes that isn't directly related to us.

The three of us had a great weekend. They were rock stars, sleeping on our air mattress on the gym floor with little heat and eating scaled-down meals. They engaged with the kids from the community and made some lifelong memories. They were amazed at the impact and influence the local church can have. Their hands got to touch each box we unloaded; I'd often pass them a box and say, "A family from our church shopped for this little girl." Or I'd remind them, "People donated these food boxes so this family could eat tonight." I worked at helping my boys see the effect our church has on so many lives. Their eyes were opened to see the church in a broader way, to see the church outside of their dad onstage. It was one of my favorite parenting moments. One of our goals as parents is to help our children create an attitude of serving the less fortunate, to develop a mind-set of thinking about and being willing to serve others.

Make ministry work for you...not against you. Because of our work schedules, our lives can sometimes look a little different from most families'. Our families often work on holidays. Even though life can be hectic during those times, make sure you still take time to create those holiday traditions for your family.

One Easter a few years ago, I (Lori) finally had a revelation. My sweet husband had preached eight services in two days and came home in walking-zombie mode midafternoon on Sunday. It being Easter, we had important family things to do. I had the kids all dressed up in their coordinating outfits, Easter baskets and plastic eggs in hand, ready for Daddy to hide the eggs for the big hunt. While he was "hiding" the eggs, I was expertly shooing the kids away from the windows. I peeked through the blinds in our kitchen to see Jud slumped in a chair on the porch, drool practically dripping from the corner of his mouth as he threw the colored eggs filled with candy into the yard to "hide" them. He was too exhausted to make the rounds of our small backyard. He looked so pitiful that I decided then and there that the important thing was not that we celebrated on Easter Sunday. The important thing was that we celebrated. If we could celebrate at a time when Daddy was more able to engage, then all the better. The Wilhite clan now celebrates Easter on Good Friday. Our kids dress up in their still-coordinating outfits, which they wear two days in a row (shhh, don't tell anyone at our church), and we head to lunch at a restaurant (because they are remarkably uncrowded that Friday), cuddle on the couch as we read the resurrection story, and then hunt eggs in the backyard (with

Dad finding all the really hard hiding places). It works beautifully for our family.

You might celebrate Christmas a little early before all the services start, or get your kids to fix you that Mother's Day breakfast in bed a day early. Remember, the important thing is that you celebrate. Make adjustments, if necessary, to ensure that you have special memories and great family time.

Give them time. Sometimes the easiest way to communicate love is by giving the gift of time, one of our most prized possessions. One of the best pieces of parenting advice we've ever heard is that no matter what you believe about how best to express love, your children will always spell love *T-I-M-E*. Schedule hours, days, or even a week of uninterrupted family time. Avoid phone calls. Let your e-mail in-box stack up. Allow the social networking world to spin on without you. Guard your days off and your evenings as best you can. Sometimes life can move at a breakneck pace; force it to slow down a bit to get great time with your kids.

Our friend Melissa Elswick, a church planter's wife in South Florida, is such an encouraging example of always putting her family first. Not ministry. Not work. Not the expectations of others. But always keeping her family before anyone else. Melissa motivates us to work hard "creatively pursuing the hearts of our children."[3] You know your children best; be creative with the time you have together. Pursue your children in ways that speak to their hearts and their individual giftings. We are called to disciple those individuals in our churches, but we must also disciple the little hearts in our homes. Ministry is a high calling, but our families are our highest calling.

Raising kids in ministry comes with its fair share of challenges. But it also comes with many more blessings. It comes with a front-row seat from which our children can see God at work in the lives of the community in which they're growing up. There will be good times and bad, but choosing to parent wisely during both the good and the bad seasons will allow our children to know God in an intimate and life-changing way. Work hard to create an environment in your churches and with your children that promotes love and acceptance. Let's help move our children from the negatives associated with being a PK to an attitude that allows them to embrace and love their role as a pastor's kid.

Shoplifting from Kmart was an incredible low point. The shame Tiffany felt made her want to run away from home. She was devastated by the consequences of her sin and knew she wanted more for her future than stolen beauty products and shallow relationships with guys. When she left home for college, she had a fresh start and determined that she would live for God and live a life of honesty.

Just like Tiffany, many pastors' kids are wandering aimlessly while suffocating under the weight of perceived expectations. Tiffany was not only raised in a pastor's home but now is a pastor's wife and mother to four beautiful kids. She has chosen to take her experiences and use them to help shape the way she parents. Her parenting philosophy hinges on the belief that giving her kids clear expectations is the most powerful thing she and her husband can do. She is determined to be the strongest voice in her kids' lives.

Ministry has been a part of Tiffany's life since the day she was born. She feels privileged to have grown up as a pastor's kid. Even in the challenging seasons, she never regretted her role. Her parents were the strongest presence in Tiffany's life. They lived a life of integrity at home; they did their best to keep ministry positive and never pressured her to do anything simply because she was the pastor's kid. Today Tiffany has more passion than ever before as she raises her four kids in this incredible life of ministry. She is committed to following her parents' lead as she and her husband deliberately guide their children through this unique life.

CHAPTER 6

Friendship and Loneliness

I get tired of everyone trying to be my friend
but really and truly not.

Confession

YOU CAN'T HAVE FRIENDS

WE'VE HEARD THAT little golden nugget of advice
hundreds of times. While we believe it is advice given
with the best intention, it is really a suffocating man-
date. It isn't, in fact, a golden nugget at all, but really
more like one of those spray-painted pebbles placed in
a "pan for gold" booth at an amusement park. False.
Deceptive. A total sham. Believing that you *must* be
alone and isolated is not only a lie but also dangerous.
Satan would love little more than a bunch of isolated,
struggling leaders. And isolation is often where we, as
leaders, find ourselves.

The relational difficulties that women in leadership

face are one of the top concerns we hear from pastors' wives and women in ministry. The questions *Who do you talk to? Who can you confide in? Who can you lean on?* can be scary. And if they are answered by a resounding *No one,* then they are downright terrifying. So let's take a look at isolation and loneliness, and delve into the hope of relational community.

Leadership, by its very nature, is isolating. To other women, we can easily become more their pastor's wife than their pal, more their boss than their buddy, and more their minister than *insert best Aussie accent here* their mate. Our friend Holly Furtick, a senior pastor's wife in North Carolina, puts it this way: We are "loved by many, but known by few."[1] People in your church surround you; ministering to and serving them, you are not known by them. Surrounded by people, you still feel alone.

Like many high school girls, the two of us had solid groups of friends...dare we say, cliques. Brandi, with her split jumps and pom-poms and her "Be aggressive. Be, be aggressive" cheers, landed herself beautifully in the oh-so-envied popular crowd. Lori, sporting an academic letter on her jacket, exhibiting the impressive ability to conjugate verbs in Latin, and spending much time in marching band, found herself, salutatorian best friend in tow, smack-dab in the middle of the nerd herd. The fun part of the nerd herd, but the nerd herd nonetheless. It's okay, she's fine with it.

With a little age, a lot of life, Brandi's loss of the ability to do a backflip, and Lori's discovery of cool jeans, the playing field evened up and cliques fell by the wayside. But a strange thing happens to leaders when they try to have friends. As Pete Wilson has been known to say, "Regular people who have close friendships are considered social. Pastors who have friends are considered cliquish." And there it is. As soon as leaders establish a network of friends—whether in their churches or outside, in their communities or out of state—that ugly word, thought to have been ditched with high school, begins to rear its ugly head. There are inevitably some people who will feel left out, hurt, jealous, or excluded.

It does not matter if your church has fifty people or five thousand, it is physically impossible to have a close, intimate friendship with everyone in it. Impossible. There are always people who wish they had a closer relationship to their pastor or are sad that they can't have lunch on a regular basis with their women's ministry director.

So we are faced with two choices as leaders. We can choose not to have friends at all. No one feels left out. No one get sad. No one gets hurt…except you, because isolation can leave you feeling beaten to a pulp. Or we can choose to have friends anyway.

A few years ago when we were interviewing Pastor Rick Warren's wife, Kay, she brought to light these simple but profound words from Paul in 2 Corinthians: *[We] opened wide our hearts to you...*[2] Kay revealed that this open-heart posture is often how we begin leadership. Hearts embracing, loving, and comforting others.[3] Before we know it, our hearts are no longer open wide, but instead are shielded, as we try to deflect those pesky rude comments, hurts, and betrayals. And if we are not careful, we will find our hearts closed tightly, boarded up like a house in the path of a hurricane, both protecting and isolating us.

When we first moved to Las Vegas, I (Lori) immediately made a connection with a new friend. I mean the throw-my-baby-shower and have-lunch-at-my-house-once-a-week kind of friend. It was great. I was so thankful and relieved to have made a connection so quickly. Over the years, the church grew and changed. New people sat in the seats, and a new core started to emerge. For people who had been around a long time and deeply loved the church, it was difficult to see it morph into something they didn't necessarily recognize.

One blistering hot July afternoon, I walked to my mailbox, feet literally burning through my thin flip-flops. I weeded through the stack of junk mail to find a letter. An actual personally written letter, can you imagine? The excitement was short-lived: I opened the envelope to find a letter from my friend—yes, my baby-shower-throwing friend. It was two pages of pain. Each line felt like a new punch to the stomach. Outlined in great detail were all the reasons she and her family were leaving the church, most unfortunately based on untrue gossip. A copy of this letter had also been mailed to each of our elders' homes. Seriously?! Not a meeting to talk about concerns? Not an inquiry into what was really going on? Nope. I just received this gross letter, which felt eerily similar to the sort of hideous breakup text a fifteen-year-old boy might send. Sending such a letter is just something you don't do.

My emotions ranged from raw woundedness to absolute fury, vacillating back and forth for days. At that point I, as a leader, had two choices, and so do you. We can choose not to have friends at all. No more hurt. No more betrayal. No more "breakup letters." Or we can choose to open our hearts wide and have friends anyway.

CHOOSING COMMUNITY

Two choices. Choosing to live in isolation like Tom Hanks stuck on that island with his sad little volleyball, Wilson, slowly going crazy with nothing but your own thoughts to keep you company. Or taking a huge risk and choosing to seek life-giving relational community. The question that always rattled around in our brains was: *Do the benefits of community outweigh the relational risk and potential hurt found along the way?* Was it worth it? Let's look at a few of the benefits of finding community in leadership.

We love this verse in Ephesians 6:18: *Keep each other's spirits up so that no one falls behind or drops out.*[4] Ever felt like dropping out of ministry? Like throwing in the towel of leadership? Ever felt like walking away from the work God has called you to? Or find yourself daydreaming about how wonderful it'd be to work at a coffee shop, bring someone their bagel, and just move on with life? We have.

This verse is clear on why community is vital in our lives. We all need people to keep our spirits up. Why? So we won't fall behind or drop out. It is vital to have encouragement, hope, and the companionship of others to walk with us through difficulty, hardship, and hurt so we can be healthier women, impacting our marriages, families, and ministries.

The difficulties, expectations, and criticism found in leadership won't go away. But if we can find people to walk through the valleys with us, to keep our spirits up, there may be a better gift than answers to questions or solutions to problems. We can have the gift of each other, which is what God intended all along.

Let's look at the story of Moses, Aaron, and Hur in Exodus 17. The Israelites were camped out in Rephidim, where there was no water to drink: a dry and dusty place where the people were "tormented by thirst" until the Lord instructed Moses to strike a rock so that water would gush forth and provide refreshment for the people. In that place, with only the Lord's provision to sustain them, the warriors of Amalek attacked. Joshua, following Moses's command, chose men to go out and fight the army of Amalek. And Moses was moved to stand at the top of the hill, gripping in his hand the staff of God that had provided the people with water to quench their thirst.

While Joshua was waging war against the Amalekites on the battlefield, Moses, Aaron, and Hur were waging war in their own way. Verse 11 says: *As long as Moses held up the staff in his hand, the Israelites had the advantage. But whenever he dropped his hand, the Amalekites gained the advantage. Moses' arms soon became so tired he could no longer hold them up. So Aaron and Hur found a stone for him to sit on. Then they stood on each side of Moses, holding up his hands. So his hands held steady until sunset. As a result, Joshua overwhelmed the army of Amalek in battle.*

There are a few things that jump out at us here. First, God is the provider of water when we are thirsty. When your soul is parched, when your spirit is weary, when you think you can't stand the desert one more minute, God can and will work miracles, sending water gushing forth in a fountain to fill you and soothe you. He can open fountains where we least expect them. He gave the Israelites a constant, abundant supply of water. He will provide for your tired soul and provide abundantly.

Secondly, God is the provider of victory when we are attacked. Our attackers may not be horse-riding, armor-bearing, sword-wielding armies. The battles may be with familiar faces armed with well-aimed verbal blows and committee meetings, or the darker spiritual battles fought in and around us. Either way, God is the provider of victory. As our friend Kerri Weems says, "Lies have a life-span, but truth endures. The truth will outlast any lies that are being told about you."[5]

And look carefully; don't miss this. God is also the provider of friends to literally hold up our arms when we cannot anymore. As women, we are often in the arm-holding business. Our husbands need us to hold up their arms on those draining, depressing Monday mornings when the "Holy Hangover" of the weekend won't let them out of its grip. As our children experience their first breakup or when the stress of hours of homework takes its toll, we lift their arms. When our friend has just discovered that her husband has been having an affair for the last few months, or debt is about to drown a woman in our Bible study, we hold up their arms. We support the arms of our coworker who just got that dreaded phone call from the doctor, and the arms of a church member who is being strangled by depression. And the list could go on. Women are arm holders.

But this passage in Exodus begs the question: *Who is holding up your arms?* Who is joining you in your pain, struggle, hurt, and weariness? Who is grabbing hold of your exhausted hands and helping to lift them to the Lord?

FINDING COMMUNITY

Sitting over a late-night dinner, a pastor friend started to break down the three kinds of people we encounter as leaders. There are the people who *want* to be your friend *because* you're the pastor's wife or ministry leader. We've all encountered these people. If you're like us, when you meet people who only want a relationship with you based on your role, you want to hightail it in the other direction. Then there are the people who *don't want* to be your friend *because* of the leadership role you play. This is actually very understandable. Inviting your boss to your birthday party can really put a damper on the fun. We get it.

But the third group of people—those are the ever-elusive ones we search for and pray for. They are the people who *want* to be your friend *despite* your leadership position. These are the friends who would just as much want to be part of your life whether you were flipping burgers or leading a church of ten thousand. It doesn't matter, because they love you for you. Finding a friend like this seems more challenging than that final page in the Where's Waldo? books, where everyone is wearing the same red-and-white-striped shirt, ski cap, and glasses. Where, in that sea of people, is she?!

The two of us have and seriously love our iPhones. They have endured apple juice spills, seen the inside of washing machines (complete with detergent and fabric softener), and ridden on the car hood during the morning school drop-off run. They are our calendars that keep our lives in order, our social networking windows that keep us in touch with friends near and far, our communication tools for both talking and typing, and they are our tiny movie screens when needed. They are incredible.

We used to think we needed friends who were like our iPhones: our one-stop, be-everything, do-everything lifelines. But this is asking people to provide what only God can supply. People aren't meant to be everything. Friends are more like fabulous apps, or to put it a little more gently, there are different types of friends and different levels of friendship.

We need great hangout friends. You know the ones. The chick-flick-watching, super-sale-shopping, cheesecake-sharing kind of friends. These friendships may not involve deep, soul-baring conversations. Nope. Need no-pressure fun time? There are friends for that. It doesn't mean that these friendships are inauthentic or not worth your time; they are friendships that meet the more surface-level need in our lives. And that's okay.

There is also a need for a closer level of friendship, a friend or two to seek parenting advice from, a friend or two who will celebrate the joys in life with us, and who will pray for us when we are struggling. No, we don't share everything. We don't talk about the challenges of leadership, or share the ministry bumps and bruises, and we may not even talk about really personal things like our marriage because of the blurry lines between friendship and leadership. But we can talk and share. There are friends for that.

But as leaders, we need another kind of friendship that allows us to share the things that we've locked away from our church members or our staff. Yes, we desperately long to "find someone who has been where we've been, who shares our fragile places, who see(s) our sunsets with the same shades of blue."[6] There are people who understand the leadership challenges we face because they faced the same challenge last week. Or women who can advise us on how to handle a sticky ministry situation because they've found themselves in the midst of a similar situation. There are friends for that.

Something really special and beautiful can happen when God knits together and binds the hearts of pastors' wives and women in ministry. We walk the same road, share the same struggles, and embrace the same calling. We need each other. These kinds of friendships "aren't about what you say, but built around what you don't have to say."[7] If you cannot find these friends at your church, look around your city. If you cannot find them in your city, by all means, search for them outside your city limits.

We are a generation of pastors' wives and leaders who are no longer limited by our geography or our ability to afford plane tickets to get to conferences. Between social networking and the incredible invention of video chat, there are opportunities to connect with women around the world who know what it is like to stand in our shoes. It takes time, energy, effort, and intentionality to make these friendships. But they are vital to our health and support as leaders who need to *keep each other's spirits up so that no one falls behind or drops out*.

No matter what level of friendship you are looking to develop, don't sit back and wait for it to come to you. Seek God and ask Him to provide these different types of friends in your life. Be proactive. Ask gals to lunch or start a Bible study with some moms at your kids' school. Start conversations with other leaders on Twitter and Facebook. Schedule a monthly time to video chat with a group of other ministry wives. Go for it. Take the risk. It is *that* important.

TO MAKE A FRIEND, YOU'VE GOT TO BE A FRIEND

When my Emma was tiny, I (Lori) never set an alarm to wake up in the morning. There was really no need to. I had a living, breathing, crying alarm clock that would dependably wake me up around seven every morning. I always had plenty of time for Emma to wake me up, get us both ready, and get to wherever I needed to be. No problem. Until, of course, I was scheduled to lead worship for our Women's Bible study one morning.

That fateful Tuesday morning, I heard the usual sounds of fussiness coming through the baby monitor next to my head. I took a deep breath, peeled open my eyes, and looked at the clock. Oh, Mercy. I was supposed to be at the church thirty minutes earlier. My sweet baby had decided this would be her first morning to discover what sleeping in until almost nine o'clock felt like.

I threw the covers off and vaulted out of bed. I ran to the closet, grabbed the first set of clothes hanging at the front, and like the Tasmanian Devil, whirled around and got those clothes on. I knew better than to look in the mirror, so I sprinted out of the bathroom, snatched Emma out of her crib (wet diaper and all), and ran to the car.

Driving like a maniac, I zipped into the church parking lot. I practically launched Emma at the nursery workers, yelling instructions about bottles, cereal, and desperately needing her diaper changed, before I took off toward the meeting room.

I walked in just as things were getting started. No

makeup. Completely frazzled. And hair sticking every which direction. The second I played that last guitar chord, I sprinted toward my husband's office. When I opened his door, his eyes bugged out a little as he took in the sight of me. He patiently listened as I rolled through the tale of my crazy morning, then gently took me by the shoulders and, with a little twinkle in his eye, said, "And your shirt is inside out, too!"

Seriously?! You've got to stinkin' be kidding me!

That's when I knew: to make a friend, you've got to be a friend. You've got to be the kind of friend who will pull someone to the back of the room and say, "Oh, girl. Poor thing, your hair looks like Einstein's. Use my brush. And for heaven's sake, borrow the loose powder I have in my purse. And bless your heart, I'll stand in front of you while you turn your shirt right side out. No way can we let you up on that stage looking like this." Yep. We've gotta be that kind of friend. So let's look at a few keys to friendship, especially when considering friendships in leadership.

First, be a protecting friend, to make a protective friend. Fight each other's battles. We believe that part of ministering together and part of friendship is choosing to speak up for one another, whether you serve on the same staff or you follow each other on Twitter.

There is a fuzzy line sometimes between what you

choose to repeat and what you choose not to repeat. You really don't need to repeat every bad thing that's said about someone to them. Sometimes people need to be aware of what's said for their own protection, but we also feel strongly that, as friends, when we hear someone talking negatively about another leader, ministry wife, or fellow staff member, it's our responsibility to take up for them. We're also called to challenge the person doing the negative talking to go to the person they have the issue with and talk through the dissension. Simple Matthew 18 action.

Part of being a friend, a sister in Christ, is fighting battles for one another, a willingness to step into the gap and stand with people who are being attacked. Hearing everything negative that is said about you is tough; surround yourself with people you know are with you, through the good and the bad. Look out for your fellow staff members, staff wives, and leaders. If you hear something that is not uplifting, confront the people who said it and think twice before you repeat it to your friend.

Be a loyal friend to make a loyal friend. *Loyalty* is a word that is thrown around a lot. In fact, it's practically a catchphrase now with businesses: "Customer loyalty is our number-one goal." How many of us have a key chain full of reward program key fobs to celebrate our loyalty? The commercial definition of *loyalty* is being loud and proud, and we believe that consumer mentality has caused loyalty in friendship to take a big hit. Consumer loyalty has allowed us to begin to believe that we'll be honored for our loyalty, when loyalty is truly a two-way street. Being loyal in relationships doesn't mean relaying all conversations that can destroy. It doesn't mean defending someone, then going to them to tell them you defended them. It doesn't mean you fill them with empty compliments and false praise. It doesn't mean standing up for people when they are around but quietly sitting by when they're not. To us, loyalty means being a friend who's safe... period.

Sometimes when people describe themselves to us as safe, we're a bit leery. *Safe* is based on experience, not verbal proclamation. Being a safe, loyal friend means being willing to have hard conversations with people who are attacking other leaders. It means being willing to confront when you see mud being slung at another woman in ministry. It means covering our friends with silence when that is the best and most helpful thing we can do for them.

Be a friend of truth and grace to make a friend of truth and grace. Healthy relationships require a balance of truth and grace. You won't live in transformational community until you make truth a part of your language. Authentic relationships require us to extend and accept grace. Often our friendships lean heavily toward grace and avoid truth. Truth causes conflict, and we prefer to avoid conflict. But oh, the gift of grace, it's a game changer.

Recently, I (Brandi) had a rather unfortunate run-in with a Toys "R" Us cashier. The exact details aren't important, but let's just say it was one of those moments we've all had when we're shocked by someone's inability. The situation extended itself into a large time frame, and my ten-minute errand turned into close to an hour. At about the forty-five-minute mark, I chose to deliver a large dose of truth to that sweet girl. Oh, I knew better; I knew I was wrong, but felt "justified" as I delivered truth. Isn't that the way it often works? We deliver truth to someone else for our own well-being, not because we're thinking about them, but because we need to get it off our chests.

If you know me at all, it'll be no surprise that the guilt ate at me. I hadn't been at home more than a few minutes when I found myself dialing up Toys "R" Us and asking for the blond cashier with the adorable headband. As I started to introduce myself, it was very clear she remembered me well. Then, as I was fumbling through my apology, my eyes filled with tears, for she forgave me with a covering of grace that blanketed my soul. Truth and grace, it's a precarious balance. To be a good friend, we have to have the ability to say the hard things with love, a healthy motive, and a heap of grace.

Be a life-giving friend to make a life-giving friend.

The always-critical, always-witty Simon Cowell is well known for quotes like "If your lifeguard duties were as good as your singing, a lot of people would be drowning" and "Shave off your beard and wear a dress. You would be a great female impersonator."[8]

For all his harsh comments, we totally love this advice given to Simon Cowell by his father: "Always remember that every single person who works with you or for you has an invisible sign on their forehead saying, 'Make me feel important.'"[9]

How can we make people feel important? Most of the time, it is the "little" things we do for people that make them feel loved, valued, and important. Don't just say you'll pray for someone; grab their hands and pray for them right then. Listen to them; really listen. Even when there are tons of people around pulling on you, take the time to listen. Shoot out a text, a direct message, or an e-mail when you are thinking of them. Or go crazy and actually mail them a real-life card.

Speak life into your friendships. In small ways and in big ways. Eyeball to eyeball and cell phone to cell phone. Make them feel important. And if we focus on being that kind of friend, God can help us make that kind of friend.

Friendships we have as adult women definitely look different than our high school friendships. We're no longer wearing our cheerleading skirts or hanging with our Latin club mates. Our current friendships take a little more work and a bit longer to build trust, but you can have friends in ministry. God created you for companionship, not isolation. We are relational beings designed to grow in community with other believers. Do the benefits of community outweigh the relational risk and potential hurt found along the way? Is it really worth it? Without a doubt, yes!

CHAPTER 7

Time and Balance

> I have no problem saying *no*. (Apparently there
> is this unspoken rule that we have to be every-
> where at all times and attend every event,
> shower, meeting, service.) I am no one's
> Savior...that would be Jesus, not me.
>
> *Confession*

WHAT BETTER WAY to begin a chapter on time and
balance than by sharing a teeny-tiny time mistake I
(Brandi) made once? Okay, it was a ginormous mistake, but I'm willing to own up to it in a printed book
that will live on for all eternity. What does that tell you
about my character? No shame, girls, no shame.

Here's the skinny. Some dear friends of ours were
getting married—a couple who had babysat for us for
several years. A couple who loved our children. A couple we would never ever in a trillion years want to
disappoint.

That Saturday morning as Pete and I were planning
our day, we had the following discussion:

Pete: What time is the wedding?

Brandi: *Five o'clock.*

Pete: Are you sure it's at five o'clock? I think it's at four o'clock.

Brandi: No, honey, I am *sure* it's at five o'clock. I am *never* wrong about a time. Trust me.

Because of a traffic-related event in our area, we arranged our child care for an earlier time than we normally would; we didn't want the traffic to make us late for this wedding. We headed out around three o'clock and arrived in historic downtown Franklin, Tennessee, around three-fifteen. At that point, we treated ourselves to Starbucks and sat on the street to people watch. The weather was gorgeous and our conversation was enjoyable. It was a very relaxing afternoon.

Around four o'clock I ventured down the street a few storefronts to check out a trendy little boutique. As I roamed through the store, I noticed they were having a denim sale. Let me stop here to interject that I love a good pair of blue jeans. I mean I adore, from the bottom of my heart, great blue jeans. Absolutely no other piece of clothing can compare to a great pair of jeans. Blue jeans with a good fit put a smile on my face. Wandering upon a denim sale, a designer denim sale at that...well, the afternoon was getting better and better.

It was about four-fifteen, and I was in the dressing

room trying on these amazing trouser jeans. I had moved into the phase of shopping where I was mentally convincing myself that I *had* to buy these as a Mother's Day gift to myself, as an investment, of course. They would surely last forever! At that point in my shopping experience, I heard my husband say, "Where is my wife?"

I said to myself, "He sounds a little frantic," so I poked my head out of the dressing room. "I'm right here, honey, what's up?"

"Get your clothes on *now*!" I hurried and pulled off the great designer trouser jeans (did I mention they were 40 percent off?) and slid back into my wedding attire. As I headed out of the boutique, I saw Pete standing on the sidewalk looking a little flustered.

"The best man just called, and the wedding started at four o'clock!" Dramatic background music began to play...okay, maybe not, but it should have, since I have never run so fast in four-inch heels.

Luckily, we were only two minutes from the church, which only made us seventeen minutes late for the wedding, at which my husband was officiating! As we pulled up to the charming little chapel, a groomsman stood in a parking place reserved for us. Pete took off in a sprint to the back of the building. The bride and her bridesmaids were standing on the front steps looking radiant as I slunk by.

I walked into the back of the chapel and spotted

several of our staff members sitting toward the front. They wouldn't have been so easy to spot, except there was this strange noise coming from their row. A noise that sounded a little like snickering! Oh, yes, our sweet, loving staff was laughing, while I was mortified that we were late for the wedding.

Fortunately, the wedding had no other interruptions, and about thirty minutes later Pete introduced our friends as Mr. and Mrs. Of course, Pete delivered the message like a true professional; I was very proud of his composure. He exited the stage and made his way through the crowd to me. I couldn't really read his facial expression and was a little worried about what he might say, so I decided to speak first.

"Honey, you did a fantastic job. In fact, my favorite part of the wedding was when you said 'Remember to love each other in good times and in bad!'"

Luckily, the families of both the bride and the groom were unbelievably gracious. They commented that they now had a wedding story to tell. Glad they have a wedding story, hate that we were the ones to provide it. And in case you're curious, I still mourn the loss of that killer pair of designer denims.

Obviously, when discussing time and balance, we're covering more than being punctual. We're focusing on the management of the time given to us in our lives. Let's take a practical look at figuring out what principles of time and balance can make your life easier.

TIME, MY NEMESIS

It's a well-known fact that the heavenly view of time is very different from our earthly viewpoint. Often life begins to swirl out of control and we start to see time as our nemesis, believing that time is working against us and toward our eventual downfall. Time is an arch-enemy ready for attack. There's just not enough time in the day to accomplish all we want to, and we become overwhelmed by all that's expected from us and by what we expect from ourselves. Let's start by looking at a challenge from Sarah Young in her well-known devotional, *Jesus Calling*.

Wait patiently with me while I bless you. Don't rush into My Presence with time-consciousness gnawing at your mind. I dwell in timelessness: *I am, I was, I will always be.* For you, time is a protection; you're a frail creature who can handle only twenty-four-hour segments of life. Time can also be a tyrant, ticking away relentlessly in your mind. Learn to master time, or it will be your master.

Though you are a time-bound creature, seek to meet Me in timelessness. As you focus on My Presence, the demands of time and tasks will diminish. *I will bless you and keep you, making My Face shine upon you graciously, giving you Peace.*[1]

Does that hit anyone else right between the eyes? There's freedom in being reminded that we are frail creatures. Freedom in being given permission to guard ourselves. We don't like to admit weakness, but we were created to handle only so much.

For those Type A personalities, the idea of *timelessness* is a little overwhelming; however, timelessness might possibly be a healthy challenge for us. Our minds don't balance productivity and timelessness well, but we should be willing to give it a try. Even as we write this, we're guilty of trying to "mentally plan" our timelessness, which obviously defeats the purpose. Our goal might just be turning time from our nemesis to our friend.

The first thing you need to know is that balance is a myth. A big, fat, *U-G-L-Y*, you-ain't-got-no-alibi myth (yes, we came dangerously close to falling back into Friday-night high school football game mode there). In fact, we kinda cringe when we hear someone ask how we "balance it all." Because we don't. We don't even come close to "all," but we do work hard to be good stewards of the time and the responsibilities that have been given to us.

I (Brandi) grew up a gymnast, so much of my focus was on balance. Performances depended on balance; safety required balance. Good balance kept me upright and protected me. Those habits carried into my adult life and have caused me to spend many hours chasing the idea of balance. Through lots of painful and frustrating trial and error, I've created a new definition for what balance really is as it pertains to managing life.

Few things relieve my mind of stress and take away tension like sweating it out at the gym. A few years ago our local gym invested in some of those flat-bottomed stability balls (I have a love-hate relationship with them). During a class one day, the instructor asked us to flip our flat-bottomed ball round side down then carefully stand on top. Supposedly, this is great for your core. I personally believe my core was ripped to shreds during pregnancy number two and there's no regaining the glory of perfect abs again, but I'm all about trying. What's interesting about these stability balls is that there's no way to actually balance. You're always shifting your weight to one side or the other, to the front, then the back, in order to maintain a vertical position. As you become more comfortable balancing on the ball, you end up shifting your weight almost imperceptibly; it's something you do without thought.

Life is often the same way. Balance in our lives is about shifting our weight where it's needed most. There will be seasons when we shift more toward ministry, then shift toward work, then shift over toward a specific relationship, and then back to home life. Managing our time is more about learning to shift our balance based on what needs our weight or our "impact" at the moment.

At times, the two of us are quite slow when it comes to e-mail. If responses require more than two sentences of thumb typing on our phones, e-mails sit for a few days, possibly even weeks, before we're able to sit down and answer. E-mails often start with "So sorry I'm slow in responding, but...." Recently, an e-mail was sent with an immediate apology referring to the effort toward "catching up and feeling on top of it." The response that came back made us laugh. It was something to this effect:

> Good luck catching up. I've been a pastor's wife close
> to thirty years, and my youngest child is twenty-three.
> Catching up still seems like the impossible.

Honestly, we really needed to hear those words. We like to feel "caught up" and on top of things. But when we pause and think about life, we do stay caught up where it's important. We stay caught up with our kids and caught up with our husbands. Relationally, we do pretty well staying caught up. So we're beginning to realize we need to focus on being caught up in the areas that matter...family, friends, relationship with God, church family. It's really all about our priorities.

How do we determine our priorities? How do we find where our weight needs to "shift" for the time being? One of our favorite exercises from senior pastor's wife Lisa Hughes is very simple and uses a T-graph.[2]

Priorities	Commitments

The graph has two labels, one *Priorities,* the other *Commitments.* Go to work, listing your priorities and your commitments on the corresponding sides. Your priorities are going to be things like God, husband, children, work, church, etc. The commitment side will include how and where your time is divided. The next step is easy yet very enlightening. Draw lines from your priorities to the corresponding commitments.

When we do this exercise, it's easy to see we're committed to boatloads of things that aren't our priorities.

And if we're painfully honest, we realize that we often shortchange our priorities (the things that are usually most precious in our lives) by giving attention to our commitments. Sadly, our commitments are often there to please someone else, not because they're a priority.

SAUCERS, PLATES, AND PLATTERS

One of the largest contributing factors to priorities and commitments is your season of life. And we daresay, season of life has a greater impact on priorities and commitments for women than it has for men. That's not intended as criticism or said with a negative heart. But for us women, our "plates" are a little different than they are for our male counterparts.

Warning: Massive Amounts of Metaphor Ahead!

We all have different-sized plates in life when it comes to our time and schedules. Some people have saucer-sized plates. They can fit a few finger foods on there, but that's about it. These people's plates are like those tiny ones you get at bridal showers, on which you can fit some grapes and a cupcake. That's it, nothing more.

Some people have gigantic platters. Platters similar to what a twenty-one-pound turkey is served on for Thanksgiving dinner. They can heap huge amounts of food on there, and none of it spills off. They have a seemingly endless amount of energy and an amazing ability to deal with lots of stuff on their platters. It's always astounding how much these people can handle.

Then there's the two of us, with our medium-sized plates. Quite a bit of food fits on there, but pretty quickly stuff starts to slip over the edges. We walk a fine line between being full and being overstuffed. But oh, how we wish to be platter girls.

As important as determining the size of your plate is determining what kinds of things are going on that plate. There are seasons of life when your plate is consumed with playdates, car-pool lines, soccer games, and helping with homework. Then there are seasons when your plate is more evenly divided among ministry, teenagers, and some semblance of a personal life. Yes, the contents of our plates will change and shift as we walk through the different seasons of life. But whether we are saucer, plate, or platter women, we need to know how and where to set limits so that things don't slip over the edges.

It's healthy to admit you have limits, to know your boundaries. There are definitely times in our lives when we find comfort in routine. The kids go back to school after a hectic and fun summer. Christmas break has ended and once again we settle into the way a "normal" day functions. However, a little too much comfort can lead to a dangerous sidekick, overcommitment. We get so used to the load we're carrying, we start to heap lots of extras onto our plates. Before we realize it, we're overcommitted.

SAY YES

How do we battle overcommitment? We must learn to create healthy boundaries. One dictionary definition for *boundary* is a line that marks the limits of an area.

We have limits. Say it with us: "I have limits." (Kinda feels good to say it out loud.) And you know what, that's okay. It's actually a good, healthy thing to realize. In order to focus on what we really love doing, to do what we feel gifted to do, we must be aware of our limits. In order to say yes well, we must also be willing to say no well.

Yes and *no* surround us daily. Emotionally charged brides *Say Yes to the Dress*. Our iPods play No Doubt, and Gwen Stefani sings "Don't Speak." We settle in front of the TV to watch movies like *Yes Man* and shows like *What Not to Wear*. *Yes* and *no* are something we see and say but often fail to act on in our daily lives. Saying yes to something means automatically saying no to something else, and we are sincere about the intention of making our yeses true yeses and our noes true noes.

Say yes to margin. Creating margin is like using new math concepts. New math is weird. It isn't what we're used to; it most certainly isn't what we grew up learning. After poring over hours of homework, learning how to add and subtract in a new way, we're convinced that *new* isn't necessarily a bad thing. Sometimes we must learn a new concept or a new way of looking at something so that our kids can get a better under-standing of math. Sometimes what was "normal" is no longer the best thing. Maybe we need to say no to what is normal, letting go of things we've always done so that we can embrace something better. When we let go of overstuffed calendars, we can embrace margin.

Often we see a free space on our calendar and we're tempted to stuff it full of activities we enjoy. There's guilt over free or empty time, but it's important to have space in our calendars. We need space in our lives to recharge, to think, to feel, to plan, and to exhale and breathe in again.

Years ago, young in ministry and marriage, Lori's husband, Jud, asked a seasoned pastor how to keep life balanced and maintain control over schedules. He was advised—in love, we're sure: "Grow up, and lead your-self. No one will do it for you. Lead yourself."

That pastor was right; no one will create margin for you. You have to look at your time, your finances, your commitments, and decide what is taking up unneces-sary space. Look back at that T-graph and see what commitment doesn't connect with your priorities. You might have to ask yourself some hard questions, as our dear friend Pastor Kerri Weems in Jacksonville, Florida, suggests:

What am I doing that isn't aligned with a spe-cific goal I have for myself, my marriage or my family?

What are 2–3 things I would cut out of my life if
   I knew I could cut it without the conse-
   quences of making someone angry?
What am I doing for others rather than for my-
   self or my family?
What is weighing me down?[3]

The most important piece of advice we've heard on
time and balance also came from Kerri, one of those
ladies who does seemingly appear to manage it all. She
shared this fantastic insight, which has really helped us
in our wrestling with time and balance: "Jesus was a
simplifier."[4] It's a simple statement, but so true, so full
of wisdom. We love the way Jesus took all 613 com-
mands and simplified them into two thoughts for us
in Matthew 22: *"Teacher, which is the most important com-
mandment in the law of Moses?" Jesus replied, "'You must
love the LORD your God with all your heart, all your soul,
and all your mind.' This is the first and greatest command-
ment. A second is equally important: 'Love your neighbor as
yourself.'"*

Love the Lord your God with all your heart and love
others as yourself. *Whoa!*

Really, it's that easy. The two of us are all about
simplicity. We're fans of systems, and we like life orga-
nized. We make efforts to keep life uncluttered, both
physically and emotionally. We work on keeping our
inner world simple and uncomplicated, as we also keep

our outer world simple and uncomplicated. But being reminded that Jesus was a simplifier has changed the way we manage life. It's changed our outlook on things both big and small, because "Love God, Love People" is what the Christian life boils down to.

> Wondering how to make an impact? Love God;
> love people.
> Trying to make a tough decision? Love God;
> love people.
> Struggling with your job? Love God; love peo-
> ple.
> Facing a trial with your family? Love God; love
> people.
> Searching for your purpose in life? Love God;
> love people.
> Evaluating what you need to dedicate more time
> to? Love God; love people.

It's such a simple concept, yet we often try to complicate it, especially when it boils down to managing time and maintaining balance.

Say yes to Sabbath. One thing we often lead our congregations and ministry organizations to do, but rarely actually do ourselves, is to participate in the Sabbath. It's not that we don't want to experience Sabbath, but the day "designated" for rest is often our busiest day of the week. What's even more fascinating is that Sabbath is a command, one of the Big Ten, yet the importance of time needed to rest and rejuvenate is often ignored.

What is Sabbath? This thought by Dan Allender gives great perspective: "Sabbath is not about time off or a break in routine. It is not a mini-vacation to give us a respite so we are better prepared to go back to work. The Sabbath is far more than a diversion; it is meant to be an encounter with God's delight."[5]

Growing up, we always related Sabbath to our Sunday dresses that twirled, and black patent shoes. From the days of Sunday school and flannel boards, we were quoting *Remember the Sabbath and keep it holy*. And like many of you, we sang many rounds of "On the seventh day God rested, He rested, God rested." Sabbath meant holding a hymnal and listening to a message delivered from behind an oak pulpit. Then we grew up and actually married pastors. Our churches looked a little different, but neither of us truly understood what practicing the Sabbath meant. It's been a learning process of living with the intention of slowing down and soaking in the goodness of God. Taking in all He has to offer as our Creator. Finding focus and rhythm to enjoy being in the presence of God.

Here is what that looks like for each of our families. Fridays are our days off and are strictly about family time. We rarely allow any church activities on those days. Oftentimes we end up at the ballpark or hitting the slides at a playground, but we're all together. We might grab dinner with friends or enjoy a family movie night. Our families are very aware that we need time together. Ministry is demanding and busy, and because of that we choose to be intentional about taking time away, unplugging with our kids. For our families, it's important to focus on large chunks of time with each other, and together encounter "God's delight."

Challenge yourselves with this question: Do your spouse and kids get the best of you or do they get the scraps left over after you're done building what you're going to build? Ouch. That question can take your breath away. It takes a tremendous amount of discipline not to cheat your family. It takes discipline to say no. It takes discipline to close the laptop and engage. It takes discipline to get out of town and unplug.

Disconnecting is tricky, but healthy disconnecting is vital. If you're thinking about Sabbath and wondering where or how to start, our friend Rick Warren, pastor at Saddleback Church, probably says it best, as his widely known Sabbath practice is to divert daily, withdraw weekly, abandon annually.

Divert daily. Find some way to divert your attention each day. It might be time spent outside among Creation. For some it's serving the less fortunate. It might be listening to your favorite worship music. You can spend time meditating and in prayer. You could engage in a hobby that feeds your soul. No matter what you choose, find a way to take a little time each day to be rejuvenated.

Withdraw weekly. Take a day off! The purpose of that day is relaxation and restoration. This is absolutely key. Everyone...every pastor, every ministry wife, every women's ministry director, every Celebrate Recovery coordinator, every worship leader...must take a day off each week. Your church and ministry will not only be fine without you one day each week, but will greatly benefit by enjoying a healthier leader the other days.

Abandon annually. Get away and abandon everything for a specified time each year. Whether you are in tents at a campground or renting a little place near a beach, abandon each year for a sabbatical. You will return to ministry rejuvenated, refreshed, and ready for whatever God has for you next.[6]

THE ART OF SAYING NO

Saying no is a necessity when saying yes to margin, yes to Sabbath, yes to our priorities, and yes to our families. Learning *how* to say no is vital.

There was a time when, if we were asked to attend a baby shower or a ministry event, we felt it necessary to launch into a well-crafted multipoint defense of why we needed to say no. In order to not hurt someone's feelings or justify our absence, we would lawyer up and bring our best case forward. Then, a couple of years ago, Kay Warren stopped us in our tracks when she said, "No is an okay word to say. You don't have to defend those kinds of choices to everybody in an effort to make them happy."[7]

What?! You can just say no and that's it? That's right. With a smile and a gracious spirit, you can look at people and just say, "No, I'm not going to be able to do that." That's it. How incredibly freeing is that?

Can you come to our small-group Christmas party? *I'm sorry; we're not going to be able to attend.*

Can you attend the graduation parties of this year's seniors? *I really wish I could, but I'm not able to be there.*

Can you stop by my Pampered Chef party...bridal shower...birthday party? *Insert sweet smile* *Nope... Can't make it...Sorry.*

We realize that your kindly put no might be met with quizzical looks and held breath as they wait for your justification for missing their special event. Just meet their eyes with a continued smile; there is no need to give excuses for time spent with your family or other ministry commitments. Learning the art of saying no was an absolute game changer for us, and it can be for you as well.

PLATFORMS AND PRIORITIES

Like many women, I (Lori) am a lover of shoes. From sparkly ballet flats to biker boots, I love what a cute pair of shoes can do to an outfit. But I've always had a special place in my heart for platforms and wedges. There is only one problem. I have serious difficulty actually walking in them.

I have fallen and bloodied my knees on many occasions. I've twisted ankles, skidded down stairs, and proven time and time again that I'm a hazard to myself wearing wedges. But there was one event that finally determined that a massive shoe purging would have to take place if I was going to outlive my cute shoes and my clumsiness.

Overstuffed with fries and a free birthday sundae, my family was walking out of Red Robin, heading to our minivan. In each hand I carried our carefully packaged leftovers, meaning there would be no fixing lunch the next day. Glory be! I was quickly following my kids, when out of nowhere, I lost my balance (I blame the wedges) and fell all the way *to my stomach* but did not drop the food. I do have priorities, people.

Sadly, my wedges went to make some Goodwill shopper very happy. But I regained my balance and maintained my priorities, which shockingly is even better than really cute shoes. Dealing with our schedules is a similar story. We can say yes to what's best, make the necessary changes, and say no to what is creating imbalance. We can pray about our lives, evaluate our calendars, refocus our commitments, and move forward toward the best God has for us.

CHAPTER 8

Criticism

I am sick of having to quietly stomach the nasty church people who slander, gossip, lie, and attack my husband and family.

Confession

GROWING UP IN our little yellow house on Harmony Street, I (Lori) lived two doors down from my best friend, Julie. In between our homes was Ray and Melba's somber-looking gray house with their two barking poodles. Though they didn't have children, Ray and Melba astonishingly didn't mind two squealing, giggling little girls carving a well-worn path in their lawn as we ran back and forth between our houses.

Julie's house seemed fancy from my limited nine-year-old perspective. It had a double-door entry and arched doorways, which seemed exotic compared to our single door and rectangular door frames. Out in the front yard, there was a two-foot-high redbrick wall outlining the grass. That little brick wall was our balance beam when we were playing "Mary Lou Retton scores a perfect 10," and our hurdle when we were doing our best Flo-Jo impersonations. The wall was the perfect backdrop for all of our 1984 Summer Olympic dreams.

We enjoyed many a warm Texas afternoon running around, jumping over, and yes, even cartwheeling on top of that brick wall. But it wasn't all fun and games. Oh, no. Unfortunately, "Mary Lou" didn't always score a perfect 10. Sometimes her foot would slip off the edge of her balance beam. Good-bye, flesh the length of your shin. Sometimes even the fastest runners tripped over the hurdles. Hello, busted knees and gushing blood.

Julie and I each had our share of war wounds. The kinds of wounds that made for wonderful stories when we were nine, but now make for ugly scars on my thirty-something-year-old legs.

In much the same way, we all have leadership war wounds. Sure, some wounds may be self-inflicted by poor choices, habits, and sin. Others may occur simply by accident, just normal jarring and bumping along the way. But many wounds come from hurt inflicted by other people in the form of criticism and betrayal. And those wounds don't leave behind faint, discolored scars on our bodies, but rather, deep, ugly scars on our hearts and in our spirits.

Critics. All leaders have them. You do. We do. Everyone does, to one degree or another. Whether you're the worship leader or the curriculum developer, the church bookstore manager or the wife of the executive pastor, critics will find you. It seems to be part of the leadership package; it's just part of the package that we would rather mark "return to sender." As Jud Wilhite has been known to say, "Everyone loves you until you lead."

RUMBLINGS

We have never been more encouraged than when it dawned on us that we have excellent company in regard to criticism.

The disciples—the men who walked the dusty roads of Israel with Jesus, reclined at tables and ate with Him, whispered to Him amongst the throngs of people, laughed and shared light, happy moments with Him, witnessed the deaf hearing their first sounds and the lame taking their first steps, experienced what it was like for water to be the only support under trembling feet, and were His closest heart-bound friends—yes, those disciples led a church where there were "rumblings of discontent."

The Bible in Acts 6:1 simply says: *But as the believers rapidly multiplied, there were rumblings of discontent.*

Have you ever heard the rumblings of discontent? They may sound like the muted rumblings of distant thunder. *The music is too loud. The room is too cold. Your husband's hair looks like he's "trying to be one of the young people."* (Yeah, that's a real one.) These kinds of rumblings are almost like background noise. Frustrating and slightly annoying, they are rumblings in the distance.

Other rumblings might sound and feel more like experiencing an F5 tornado directly overhead while you are huddled in the corner, arms covering your head. Deafening. Hurtful. Destructive. *The teaching isn't deep enough. You don't even preach the Bible here. If you were really a woman of God, you would do what I want you to do. The leadership here isn't Godly.*

When we read Acts 6:1 again, *But as the believers rapidly multiplied, there were rumblings of discontent,* God whispers to our hearts: "You aren't alone." Leaders, from the beginning of the church, have heard rumblings.

Criticism and rumblings of discontent usually stem from one of a few different places.

Critiques, not critics. No one likes a critic. But as our friend Tricia Lovejoy, a church planter's wife, says, we can all benefit from a trusted friend speaking truth into our lives, even if it's uncomfortable at times.[1] We must be willing to listen with a receptive heart. In times of loving, helpful critique, we must refuse to be offended and resist assuming a defensive attitude. We all know that being receptive to constructive criticism can make us better.

There is a difference between critics and critiques. You must strive to find people in your life whom you trust, who have your best interests at heart, and who love the Lord. Then be open to the accountability and improvement they can provide.

"It's nothing personal, but…" Oh, those four little words. Just reading them is almost cringe inducing. They are most often immediately followed by some kind of verbal head-butt. These words are never fun and are usually personal for both the speaker and the leader. These are usually issues of personal preference.

Pastor Kerri Weems at Celebration Church recently pointed out that "when [critics] say it's not personal, they mean it, but not in the way you think. They mean it's not personal about YOU. It is, however, personal about THEM." She then gave the following examples:

They might say, "The teaching isn't deep enough." But what they really mean is, "I really enjoy expository teaching, and this wasn't a good fit for me."

They might say, "People are not empowered to serve there." But what they really mean is, "I wasn't good enough to lead worship, and that hurt."

They might say, "I just couldn't get connected to anyone there." But what they really mean is,

"Big crowds make me uncomfortable and over-whelmed. I need to be in a smaller church."

They might say, "The pastor and his wife are so stand-offish." But what they really mean is, "I miss the close relationship I had with my previous pastors, and it makes me sad that I might not be able to have that here."[2]

That's so true, isn't it? In an effort to verbalize a personal preference, people often convey things in a hurtful, critical way, not even realizing how much those comments can hurt our hearts, because they don't have the same kinds of ties to the ministry that those of us who are leaders do. They haven't com-mitted their lives to serving Jesus by working in His church, spent hours upon hours in prayer over the smallest details of the organization, or invested their time and energy at such a high level. But as leaders, we have, which is why these criticisms are so incredibly personal to us.

We always thought that if we had a ready answer in our heads, we could handle these nothing-personal situations a bit better. Our usual answer, in our super-sweetest voices, is "...for you."

We've found that it works in myriad situations, little ones and big ones.

"The music is too loud."...for you, but there are others who enjoy the music at that volume.

"It is too cold in the auditorium." . . . for you, but did you see our poor worship leader and the sweat pouring off his head?

"The teaching isn't deep enough." . . . for you, and—oh yeah—that is totally and completely personal.

Conviction isn't comfortable. We can't think of one time when the Holy Spirit has been convicting us when we have been comfortable. Not once. In fact, the discomfort He allows is part of what spurs action.

We've noticed, though, that for some, instead of responding to conviction with action, they respond by lashing out at others. A bit of shooting-the-messenger syndrome.

For instance, anytime there is a giving series at church, criticism emerges. As soon as you start to talk about people's pocketbooks, comments like "The church is just after our money!" start to fly around. Those critical comments don't come from people who are living in obedience to the generosity God is calling His people to. Nope. Those the Holy Spirit is working on and convicting are the ones who lash out. Conviction is not comfortable. At all.

When it comes to criticism, we cannot personalize someone's Spiritual issue between the Holy Spirit and them. Yes, the mud may be slung in our direction, but many times it is between them and the Lord. Our responsibility is to share Truth and let the Holy Spirit move, no matter what comes back in our direction.

Hurting people hurt people. If you've been in ministry very long, you've heard this a million times, and have used it to comfort yourself after opening and reading a nasty letter, going head-to-head with someone in the church lobby, or having someone you've helped over and over turn and betray you.

We've heard and said "hurting people hurt people" so many times that it has almost lost its impact and edge. So let's look at how Richard Rohr puts it: "If you do not transform your pain, you will surely transmit it to those around you and even to the next generation."[3]

It doesn't matter if we've been believers two months, two years, or twenty-two years, if we do not let God do His redemptive work in transforming our pain, we will certainly transfer it to others. Sometimes, as leaders, we are on the receiving end of someone's untransformed pain—the pain of their past, the pain of their broken family, the pain of their financial situation, the pain of loneliness.

Understanding some of the roots of criticism doesn't necessarily make harsh words and critical comments hurt less. It can, however, impact how we respond to others and react out of that hurt. As Pete Wilson says: "Hurting people hurt people. Hurting leaders hurt *lots* of people." So let's take a look at our reaction to criticism.

AN ANSWER WITH A DASH OF ATTITUDE

I (Lori) was sitting all by my lonesome, as usual, in my front-row spot. About halfway through service, a lady sauntered in and joined me in my deserted row. I was glad for the company, since it can be a little isolating up there, surrounded by empty seats.

My husband preached about something that I can't even remember now but I'm sure was brilliant. I laughed at all his jokes and stories and nodded at all the right moments.

As soon as service came to a close, the lady walked over to me and asked, "Do you go to this church all the time?"

Smiling sheepishly, secretly excited not to be recognized as the pastor's wife, I answered, "Why, yes. Yes, I do."

She shot back: "Then maybe you can tell me why they don't pray at this church!"

Whoa, Nelly! Huh?! Where in the world did that come from?

Cue smile, and sweetest voice: "Well, he just prayed at the close of service just now."

She huffed at me: "Well, if you call that little quip a prayer!"

Cue deep breath, forced smile, and attempt at a sweeter voice as I pointed out the different times of prayer during the service, including the ones she had missed since she'd been late. I reminded her about the team of people that is ready, willing, and able to pray with individuals after service.

We volleyed back and forth for several minutes, until I had had enough. I put my hand up in that talk-to-the-hand fashion and said (with a dash of attitude, minus the sweet voice): "You know what, that is my husband. I'm not sure what you want me to say right now. I'm obviously not able to say what you want to hear."

I heard a sharp intake of breath, and her eyes got really big. Then she quickly took off like a throng of Black Friday shoppers as soon as the doors open at 2 AM at Target. Boom. Gone. I stood there for a moment to get myself calmed down before I went to visit with some people. I was in the middle of talking to someone a few minutes later when she showed up with tears in her eyes and said sternly: "Sorry, but you don't have to be so defensive."

Defensive. Really?! I stood there for five minutes, nodding, smiling, talking sweetly, while I listened to you rant about our church and my husband. Yeah, I finally got a little defensive, but you have no idea how much I was holding back, lady!

Part of me wished I could get my little dash of attitude back. But part of me was just glad to get that whole situation stopped. It was getting nowhere fast.

The truth is, there have been times in both of our ministries when we've spent more time worrying about how people would respond to something our husbands said from the stage than we've spent praying for God to move in people's lives and hearts. Times we've anguished over an offhanded comment made in the middle of the lobby rather than giving the benefit of the doubt and extending forgiveness. Times we've considered sneaking out of town rather than fighting a hard battle that we know we've been called to fight. Times we've allowed fear to drive our motives rather than the battle for lost souls.

In those times we have to stop and think, "Who is the enemy?" Are we fighting the elders? Critical church members? Wrong impressions? No, our enemy is the one who comes to kill, steal, and destroy—destroy the calling God has on our life and the joy we find in that calling.

Don't let critics take your calling. It's been said that many people leave ministry because of a handful of critical people. Don't let someone or even a handful of someones steal the calling that Almighty God has placed on your life. They cannot have it. Cling tightly to the mission and leadership God has given you.

Don't let critics steal the joy from ministry. Sure, ministry is tough. It would be easy to come up with a list of the tough stuff. But oh, there are so, so many things that are wonderful. There is so much to celebrate, enjoy, and love. Don't let the negative overshadow the great things that God is doing. Don't let them steal your joy.

God has put you in this place and in this moment. In the midst of criticism, He will not leave you alone. As you cling to the calling He has on your life, He will not abandon you. There's a verse in Isaiah that we're learning to turn to in times of fear, in times of battle, and in times when momma-bear instincts kick in: "For I hold you by your right hand—I, the LORD your God. And I say to you, 'Don't be afraid. I am here to help you.'"[4] We face no challenges alone and receive no criticism in isolation. No battles are fought as a single soldier.

POISON OR FRUIT

The two of us are sensitive people. As hard as we have tried to become thick-skinned and put on a strong face, deep down we're still sensitive to criticism. However, as sensitive as we are to other people's words, we often don't realize the impact our words might have on others. We're not as careful with our words and the tone they carry. We sometimes forget that, as Andy Stanley, pastor at North Point Community Church in Alpharetta, Georgia, says, "our words weigh a thousand pounds."[5] As leaders, our words carry more weight with those around us. They can lift people to great heights, and they can pulverize others. God desires our words to bring life.

About halfway through my pregnancy with my second son, I (Brandi) was onstage helping with one of the elements in our service. During the second trimester, I still usually felt pretty good about myself and had in fact squeezed into a pair of nonmaternity jeans, using a rubber band to buckle them, and was sporting a roomier nonmaternity shirt. I knew I obviously looked pregnant, but I didn't look like a whale—or so I thought. After the service, I was approached by a couple I knew fairly well, Kathy and Jeff. Kathy started our conversation the way most people do in the South, with a hug, then proceeded to tell me how cute I looked (little did I know she was gearing up for a doozy of a comment).

After I thanked her, she went on to say, "When I first saw you from the front I couldn't believe how good you looked—in fact, I didn't think you looked pregnant at all. But then you turned around, and I saw your backside and thought to myself, 'Well, she obviously gets pregnant on her rear end first.'" Yes, she went there, and she smiled the whole way through. I'll be honest; it took all the self-control I had to keep my jaw from hitting the floor. I was in shock that those words had actually come out of her mouth. I was hurt, felt uncomfortably mammoth, and wanted to spew some venom right back at her.

But here's what I knew about Kathy that most people didn't: she was battling infertility. A baby was what

Kathy wanted more than anything else in this world. She and her husband had tried for years to get pregnant; it was the one prayer she took to God repeatedly. You know when you buy a new car, and you think you're purchasing something unique? As soon as you drive off the car lot, every other car you pass on the road is identical to yours. Well, I'm sure that's how Kathy was feeling. She couldn't walk through the mall without passing pregnant women. Every hostess at a restaurant seated her next to pregnant women and every client at work had somehow gotten pregnant at the same time. And now she showed up to church, sat down where she hoped to leave her anguish, and up popped a pregnant gal onstage. It wasn't that Kathy didn't like me or wasn't happy for me, she just didn't know how to package her words.

Often the way we say something is as important as what we say. The same set of words can be delivered in two totally different ways, one that fires the words back as an insult or the other, which delivers words speaking life into a situation or person. It's very similar to receiving a gift. Let's say two gifts are placed in front of you. The gifts are exactly the same, but the presentation is vastly different. The first gift is presented in a crinkled brown paper bag that's been stapled shut. The second gift is elaborately wrapped—the paper is beautiful, the bow exquisite, and the gift tag is signed with love. When given the choice, we'd all go with the more embellished choice, even though on the inside, the gifts look exactly the same. Our words are very similar: so much emphasis is put on what we say, but we need to put more focus and prayer into how we say them, how we present our words. Your words matter. They carry weight. Your delivery of words is tremendously crucial. As Proverbs 18:21 says: *Words kill, words give life; they're either poison or fruit—you choose.*[6]

And because I know you're all curious, I'll tell you that my response to Kathy was very gentle. I stuffed down the venom, took a deep breath, and patted Kathy on the back. Then I smiled and told her, "Now, Kathy, some comments you should only say to Jeff on the car ride home. Y'all have a great week." Then I turned and waddled down the hallway.

When determining the packaging of our words, it's best to be aware of others' needs. In order to do that, we need to spend more time being in the moment— choosing to be attentive, listening, and understanding; viewing our words as the powerful tool they are and processing the impact they have. Just think of the power behind these words.

I'm sorry.
You're forgiven.
I love you.
I'm proud of you.

You *can* do it.

I'm glad you're a part of this team.

Encouragement is simply inspiring others with courage or pouring courage into them. We don't know about you, but there are days when we could certainly use an extra dose of courage. So don't be shy, go pour some courage into someone else.

TAKING THE HIGH ROAD

We've often sat cuddled up on couches with our teary-eyed children, listening to stories of fights with friends and hurtful words hurled on the playground. Gently, we remind them not to try to get even, but instead, to take the high road—taking the high road being a conscious decision to do the right thing, to stay above-board, to ignore their own selfishness and choose to be honorable, to do what's right even if it doesn't benefit them directly.

Simply, to be the better person.

But sometimes being the better person isn't natural, not for our heart-hurt kids, and not for us as grown women, either. Defending ourselves, explaining our actions, and even joining in the negative behavior are all natural reactions. We learned a long time ago that the high road is the only path worth taking, but we've failed in that more than a few times. Sometimes "issues" are going on around us, and we simply get our feelings hurt.

Here's where we failed ourselves and those around us: we let our feelings stay hurt. Thoughts of ourselves and our hurt continually replayed in our minds. Failing to pray it through or immerse ourselves in the Bible, we basically ignored our own responsibility in the "issue" and just felt sorry for ourselves. However, by our doing so, Satan was able to latch on to something we were struggling with, gain a foothold, and have it delivered on a silver platter.

So today, regardless of what roadblocks you face—the negative thing said about the ministry project you've been working on, the "parenting advice" that woman just *had* to share with you in the church parking lot, the collection that the women's Bible study took up to buy new clips, bows, and headbands for your daughter, since you don't do her hair the "right way," the betrayal by your closest friend—remember to take the high road. Trust us, it's the only path worth taking.

We love this anecdote that author Linda Dillow shares about Clara Barton, founder of the American Red Cross. Clara was reminded of a vicious deed someone had done to her years before.

"Don't you remember it?" her friend asked. "No," came Clara's reply, "I distinctly remember forgetting it." She had made a conscious choice to forgive a vicious deed, a conscious choice to continue forgiving when reminded of the deed. By replying, "I distinctly remember forgetting it," Clara Barton was saying, "I remember choosing to forgive, and I *still* choose to forgive."[7]

When we run into the critical person while at the grocery store, when the family who painfully left our church chooses to come back as if nothing happened, when we hear a third party discussing our hurt and our pain, it is imperative to distinctly remember to forget. It is not a one-time act, but a gift we must choose to continue to give. Sometimes we will have to choose to forgive and forget, and forget again, and distinctly choose to forget over and over again.

KEEP YOUR CHIN UP

When it comes to music, Brandi passionately loves her country music and publicly shares her affection for Keith Urban. Lori's more a U2 girl and would never miss a local Jack's Mannequin concert. We talk music, burn CDs, and even build ringtones around favorite songs. But one thing we've never done together is sing karaoke. There's no doubt that when the day comes when we get to break out the karaoke together, our playlist will include the song "Mean" by one of our favorite theologians, Taylor Swift.

When asked about the song written to her critics, Taylor replied, "There's constructive criticism, there's professional criticism, and then there's just being mean. And there's a line that you cross when you just start to attack everything about a person...This happens no matter what you do, no matter how old you are, no matter what your job is, no matter what your place is in life, there's always gonna be someone who's just mean to you."[8]

She's right, people can sometimes just be downright mean. Criticism is going to happen; it's unavoidable. Keep in mind that you don't want to take on someone else's personal preferences, spiritual issues, or untransformed hurt. Keep watch over your response, both in words and in reactions. When you do those things, you'll be able to keep your chin up when criticism inevitably comes your way.

CHAPTER 9

Burnout and Discouragement

I battle depression on a daily basis but am expected to keep pressing on.

Confession

DEAD BATTERY

BRANDI LIVES IN the faraway land known as Music City, Nashvegas, aka Nashville. I (Lori) live in Sin City, the Entertainment Capital of the World, aka the real-life Vegas. Getting to hang out eyeball to eyeball is a rare treat. Our friendship depends heavily on phone calls, text messages, video chats, and tweets. The infrequent occasions when we are in the same town mean incredibly late nights, lots of laughing, and talking about five different subjects simultaneously.

Saturday night in Vegas can be a unique adventure, to say the least. Thousands of people navigate the Strip, walking on sidewalks littered with strip club "business" cards and weaving between people dressed up as Captain Jack Sparrow and others yelling into bullhorns demanding that people repent. So when Brandi was visiting one smokin' hot August Saturday, we decided to hit the town and take on the craziness—in an appropriate pastors' wives kind of way, of course. I ditched my mommy minivan for my husband's much cooler cherry-red Mustang. We were looking pretty cute, Brandi in her skinny white pants and wedge sandals, me in my faux rattlesnake heels. We ate a great dinner, acted silly, and laughed a lot.

We hopped into the Mustang, ready to leave the restaurant; I stuck the key in the ignition. Nothing. Nada. Zip. Zilch.

We grabbed the nearest valet guy, since they are available at almost every turn down on the Strip, and asked him to jump the car. While we waited for him to come up with some kind of vehicle to use to help us out, we decided to move the car, which was pinned in on both sides in the parking garage. In our wedges and rattlesnake heels, we started pushing. It was great as long as the car was heading down the ramp, but when we looked at the incline we would need to push the car up to get it out of the way, we knew that it was better to just leave it in the middle of the road.

Then, like a knight in shining armor driving the world's largest truck, the valet guy came to our rescue.

He hooked up the jumper cables, let it charge for a few seconds, and tried to start the car. Nothing.

"We'll give it a couple of minutes," he confidently said. And of course we had absolute faith in our new-found hero.

In the meanwhile, two different couples whose cars were blocked, not only by my little Mustang but also now by the giant Ford truck, came out. We had a nice chat as we tried to charm them so they wouldn't be angry that we were all sweating it out in a steamy parking garage. When the valet tried to start my car again...zipola.

Five more minutes of charging with another set of "better" jumper cables led to...wait for it...nothing.

Time to break in those cute shoes again, this time with help from all our new friends. We pushed the car up the incline and back into its space. My husband Jud came to our rescue, driving us home until the battery could be replaced. Nothing but the best Vegas adventures when my friends come to town.

The desert is notoriously hard on batteries. Even the superamazing seven-year car batteries seem to last only about three years. The combination of the heat and the kind of dryness that makes you feel as if you need to bathe in lotion is fatal for car batteries.

Leadership and ministry are tough, too. Heat? Check. Inclement weather? Check. Bumps, bruises, and exhaustion along the way? Check. One day you're able to start up and go just fine. The next, you can't even get your engine to turn over. You're dead. Worn out. Done.

In this chapter we are going to look at the emotional journey, the ups and downs, that can be part of leadership. We're also going to get some insight into keeping burnout and discouragement at bay, because none of us wants to get caught trying to push a dead or dying ministry up an incline in our cute heels.

In ministry the word *burnout* is used quite often, and burnout is a big contributing factor to discouragement and depression. What often leads us to burnout is stretching ourselves too thin without recharging. Between volunteering, plugging all the empty holes, parenting, and loving our husbands, often we're not thinking about ourselves. Julie Richard, a senior pastor's wife in Austin, once told us, "I think the toughest part of ministry for me has been in those times when I wasn't loving ministry, when I wasn't pumped to go to church. I knew that my kids were following my lead, and I was doing my best to choose to love it. I knew that my disease, my frustration, was just as contagious as my enthusiasm and excitement about our ministry. That's when I had to determine what my limits were, what the signs were that I needed a little vacation and refueling time. Again, I had to listen to God's whispers and not the whispers, murmurs, expectations of others. Now that I've been doing this awhile, I know

how to pace myself and how to schedule refueling/
refreshing/replenishing time, time away with my husband, time away with our family, time away with other
pastors and their wives, and time away with my pastors' wives' friends! Refueling our tanks is what keeps
us in the race, and I want to be in this race all the way
to the finish line!"[1]

Julie is so right: knowing ourselves and our limits is
what helps us avoid burnout. Following through with
time for reflection and refueling keeps us from being sidelined. Maybe what we need during times of
burnout is some good old-fashioned rest. A few days
or weeks away from the pressures of leadership and
the community. Whether you're in a tent, grilling hot
dogs over a campfire in the mountains, or burying
your toes in the warm sand while listening to the waves
roll in, time to rejuvenate and recharge the battery can
go such a long way in helping overcome those inner
battles.

DISCOURAGEMENT AND DEPRESSION

Emotions are a part of ministry. There's enthusiasm
when all goes according to plan. Joy when a life is
changed by the power of God. Discouragement when
the unexpected occurs. Pain when a family leaves the
church. Uncertainty. Anticipation. Love. Concern. Ap-
preciation. Indifference. Often in ministry the focus
is on outer victories, successful ministries, growing

churches, life changes of those people we're reaching out to. But when we talk about the emotional journey of ministry, it's important to stop and focus on winning the inner battles of our hearts and spirits. Outer victories mean nothing if we don't win the inner battle.

When our batteries die, we are waging an inner battle against burnout, discouragement, and depression. Can you relate to any of these feelings, originally pointed out to us through Pastor Tom Holladay, from Saddleback Church, which we've heard echo from many women in leadership over the years?

I want to run. At times, the combination of physical and emotional fatigue makes you feel like escaping. Everyone around you may be celebrating, but you can think of nothing better than hightailing it out of leadership. When you're run-down, you want to run away.

I've had enough. You may have said, "I've reached my limit." You are done. We've had so many women leaders tell us they've had enough. They are ready to walk away from leadership or leave ministry completely.

I'm all alone. No one can relate. I'm the only one who has faced this struggle. When you decide you're all alone, the inner battle is almost lost. With isolation being such a major challenge in ministry, Satan often uses these thoughts, hoping to defeat us.[2]

A Walgreens parking lot in the middle of the day is

a bustling place. Cars coming and going. People zipping into the store to grab some medicine to help kick their allergies, or to process the family photos from the birthday party over the weekend, or to buy a couple of items they saw on sale in the Sunday paper. In the midst of all the commotion outside her car window, an empty bottle of wine in her lap, Heather sat and formulated a plan. She would drive herself to the highway, propel her car over the edge, and end it. End the pain. End the hurt. End the addiction. End. It. All.

Heather had been in ministry with her husband for two years. The fast pace of leadership suited her. A cram-packed schedule meant no time to think about hurt, childhood trauma, and feelings of inadequacy. The attempt to be everything to everyone meant that very little was left to care for herself. And that seemed fine, for a while. But you can hold a buoy underwater only so long before it will force its way to the surface again.

She began drinking in secret, attempting to numb what was right below the surface. The overcommitment and drinking just weren't enough to keep all that hurt and brokenness at bay. So she sat in that Walgreens parking lot, having finished off her newly purchased bottle of wine, and called her husband to say good-bye.

Heather completely broke down. She began to hit

her head repeatedly on the steering wheel. Over and over. Banging her head. Again and again.

Bloodied, bruised, and having sustained a concussion, Heather looked up and locked eyes with her husband, paramedics, police, and firefighters. As she was being pulled from her car, Heather went into combat mode: kicking and screaming, fighting those who were trying to help save her life. Six men worked together to get her strapped down, tranquilized, and transported to the emergency room and then to a psychiatric ward.

Wearing a hospital gown and allowed to keep only her socks, Heather found herself alone, crazy, and a pastor's wife locked in a tiny cell.

Some polls state that up to 88 percent of pastors' wives struggle with periods of depression.[3] Even if you haven't fought times of depression, we all have certainly faced times and seasons of discouragement and feeling overwhelmed.

We love the Psalms. They are such a raw, real look at the emotional ups and downs David faces. In one Psalm, he will be dancing in jubilation, and in the very next, he'll be crying out in sorrow. Hills and valleys. Peaks and pits. Look at Psalm 9:1–2: *I will thank you, Lord, with all my heart, I will tell of all the marvelous things you have done. I will be filled with joy because of you. I will sing praises to your name, O Most High.* Just a few verses later in chapter 10:1: *O Lord, why do you stand so far away? Why do you hide when I need you the most?*

Ever been there? Ever had seasons of bliss and elation give way to dismay and despair? Times when you were fired up and ready to go, but then, out of nowhere, your emotional battery died, and you just couldn't seem to get it jump-started again? We've been there, and so has the psalmist. Let's take a look at Psalm 42 and see what God might have to say to us.

Day and night I have only tears for food, while my enemies continually taunt me, saying, "Where is this God of yours?"

My heart is breaking as I remember how it used to be: I walked among the crowds of worshippers, leading a great procession to the house of God, singing for joy and giving thanks amid the sound of a great celebration!

Why am I discouraged? Why is my heart so sad? I will put my hope in God! I will praise him again—my Savior and my God!

Now I am deeply discouraged, but I will remember you—even from distant Mount Hermon, the source of the Jordan, from the land of Mount Mizar. I hear the tumult of the raging seas as your waves and surging tides sweep over me.

But each day the LORD pours his unfailing love upon me, and through each night I sing his songs, praying to God who gives me life.

"O God my rock," I cry, "why have you forgotten me? Why must I wander around in grief, oppressed by my enemies?"

Their taunts break my bones. They scoff, "Where is this God of yours?"

Why am I discouraged? Why is my heart so sad? I will put my hope in God! I will praise him again—my Savior and my God!"

TEARS FOR FOOD

I (Brandi) love food, but I never experienced weird food cravings during any of my three pregnancies; instead, I experienced food obsessions. With each of my pregnancies I developed an obsession with one particular food and couldn't get enough of it. With Jett, it was meat loaf. I can't begin to tell you how much meat loaf I ate. I'd cook meat loaf, mashed potatoes, and peas just for myself, eat a huge helping, and then save those precious leftovers for breakfast the next morning. There was no such thing as too much meat loaf. During Gage's pregnancy, I became hyperfocused on avocado. Avocado in any form and on any food. I remember once taking a cheap frozen pizza out of our oven and dipping it into guacamole. It was heavenly. When I was pregnant with Brewer, the infatuation was potato salad. I've been a potato salad fan for years, but during my final pregnancy potato salad danced around in my mind, tempting me at every meal. I'd smear it on bread and make potato salad sandwiches. I'd bake it and always add extra brown spicy mustard. I spent those nine months on a carb binge.

What about these cravings? Pickles dipped in brownie mix. Cheese and peanut butter sandwiches. Drinking pickle juice like it's Kool-Aid. Broccoli and mint jelly sandwiches. Cheese Whiz and jelly. Fries with mustard and hot sauce. Soap. Self-rising flour and crushed ice.

Gross? Yes. But all of these are documented crazy pregnancy cravings.

But what about a craving for tears? Have you ever been so down and discouraged that the only thing you could stomach was the saltiness of your own tears? You aren't alone. Again, the psalmist says, *Day and night I have only tears for food... Why am I discouraged? Why is my heart so sad?*

Maybe your schedule has you stretched too thin; it seems as if you haven't seen your family in months. Criticism might be so thick and painful you can't see any light on the other side of that darkness. Perhaps the elders of the church are meeting about your husband's job this week. You're hurt. You're scared. You're discouraged. It could be that you are choked by isolation and loneliness. You feel you can turn to no one, talk to no one, share with no one. Maybe your close friends and core volunteers are leaving the church. You may have been called to a new ministry in a new city and feel completely overwhelmed by the prospect of starting over.

Your heart may be broken. You may have only tears

for food right now, but you are not alone. The psalmist was there. We've certainly been there. Most women in leadership have been there at one point or another. And most important, God, the collector of our tears, is with you even now.

Just remember that through the ups and downs of your journey, you must continue to feel. Don't allow tough situations and harsh critics to get the best of you and callus your heart. We know that tears are painful, and we've lived in fear that if we allowed our floodgates of emotion to open, the tears might not stop. But let us tell you what is even scarier—numbness. Guarding yourself, shielding your emotions until you feel nothing at all, is even worse. One of people's main forms of self-preservation is our tendency to go numb in order to avoid the pain, *but we encourage you to always continue to feel your way through life.*

WANDERING IN GRIEF

A few years ago, I (Lori) found myself 1,050 miles away from our families, with a precious six-month-old little girl and a husband who was trying to find his way in his new ministry role. I felt very lonely, locked away in fear of the expectations of others and myself. Insecurity grabbed hold of my heart. I knew beyond the shadow of a doubt that my husband, Jud, was called into ministry. I knew what his gifts were, and what Jud was supposed to do with his life. But deep down, I wondered if God had made a mistake with me. Surely He didn't really mean for small, insignificant, normal me to be married to such an amazingly gifted pastor. There must have been some kind of error.

First I started to wander down negative trails, then later down the paths of discouragement and depression. As Psalm 42 says, I *wander[ed] around in grief*. I wandered in the grief of being separated from our family, friends, and support system. I wandered in the grief of being placed in an unhealthy church. I wandered in the grief of inadequacy. I wandered.

Most days it felt as if someone had shut the light off in my life. I felt dark and numb, but I was a master faker. I could slap on a smile and fool the women in my Bible study or say the right words and trick my friends. I could stuff my thoughts and emotions so deep I could fake out my husband...well, almost.

After a year of emotional stuffing and suffering, my body started to push back. Finally, after living with a migraine for about six weeks, I went to see a doctor. I was miserable. I had had enough. The doctor listened to me talk and sob for a while before prescribing depression medication. I drove home, prescription in hand, in complete shock. Was this darkness I had wrestled more than discouragement? Was this joyless numbing I felt really depression?

Jud and I went for a long walk in the park. Having faced the depression that was really going on in my life, I felt a torrent of thoughts and emotions starting to gush out of me. It was the first time I had talked to my husband about how difficult our move had been and how much I feared I would negatively impact his ministry. Bringing to light what I had fought to keep secret was the first step toward getting emotionally healthy again. It certainly didn't happen overnight. But God started His work on the reopening and re-softening of my heart.

I had to cling to the Sovereignty of God. I trusted that we were not in our roles or situations by accident, but instead by His design and for His purpose. I grew to believe that He knows every fault and every weakness I have, but still called me to be married to my husband and called us to His church.

I tried to get honest and authentic with those closest to me about my struggles and feelings. No more hiding. No more faking. Allowing people into my struggle enabled them to speak into my life—not for false flattery or puffery, but they spoke God's truth over me and into me. They strengthened my faith and poured courage into me when I needed it. I had spent too many years alone and isolated with my own thoughts rattling around in my head, instead of allowing those thoughts to be challenged by others with their wisdom and with their love.

I started to talk to myself. No, not crazy ramblings spoken to myself out loud. D. Martyn Lloyd-Jones said to talk to yourself more than you listen to yourself.[4] He meant that when I hear that voice inside my head that tells me I am not worthy or that I'm less than I ought to be, I can counter it by speaking God's Word to myself. I don't allow those negative messages to play, and replay, and replay again in my mind, but instead I remind myself that the Lord knows the plans He has for me. They are good plans and not plans for disaster. Plans to give me a future and a hope. I remember that I am fearfully and wonderfully made, and that all of His works are *wonderful*. And that, according to Ephesians 2:10: *We are God's masterpiece. He has created us anew in Christ Jesus, so we can do the good things he planned for us long ago.*

My feet found new paths. Not those of negativity, discouragement, and depression, but paths of freedom and joy as I learned to stop wandering in grief and to embrace hope in the Lord.

REMEMBER AND HOPE IN THE LORD

I (Brandi) have two very vivid memories from early childhood. The first is going to the hospital with my dad to pick up my mom and new baby brother. I distinctly remember walking down the long corridor and waiting on a bench by double doors. I waited for what seemed like a lifetime, because back in those days siblings weren't allowed to visit new babies, and for a four-year-old who hadn't seen her momma in four days, anything over thirty seconds seemed like an eternity. Then those doors were pushed open and out came a wheelchair holding my mom and my itty-bitty brother. I was mesmerized by him and those tiny hands and feet.

The other memory happened about a year later and was almost as exciting as a new baby brother; I attended my first concert, by Barbara Mandrell. My parents got a babysitter for my brother, and we drove to the Christian County Fair. My life was forever changed as my love for country music began. I stood in the empty aisle and sang at the top of my lungs, "You can eat crackers in my bed anytime, baby" (which was entirely appropriate, because truly wasn't she just eating Ritz and chatting with friends?). On the edge of my seat, I belted out, "I was country when country wasn't cool" until I was hoarse. A fan was born.

Warm, fuzzy memories are great. They usually bring a smile to our face and a little pep to our step. But oddly enough, there are times when remembering the good ol' days can also break our hearts. Can you relate to this part of Psalm 42? *My heart is breaking as I remember how it used to be: I walked among the crowds of worshippers, leading a great procession to the house of God, singing for joy and giving thanks amid the sound of a great celebration! Why am I discouraged? Why is my heart so sad?*

In seasons of struggle, heartache, and discouragement, we can be tempted to look back and remember the feelings we used to have when we were closer to God or when life seemed brighter. You remember feeling great joy as you led other women in worshipping God. You reminisce about the delight you once felt when you taught Bible study. Feelings of love and hope come to mind when you recall how vibrant your prayer life used to be. And it breaks your heart. You would love nothing more than to have those feelings again.

The problem is that our feelings can be fickle, and we've got to dwell upon much more than our feelings. We must dwell upon God and fix Him in our minds. Choose worship, and experience a fresh encounter with Christ.

Even when it feels as if miles of wasteland stretch between us and God, we must remember Him. Remember His goodness. His mercy. His forgiveness. His pursuit of us. His incredible love. His radical grace. His faithfulness. His presence even when we are distant.

You may feel as if God is not with you or does not hear you in the midst of your struggles. You may feel as if your cries for help are merely bouncing off your ceiling. However, the truth of the Bible is that God is always powerfully at work in our lives—even when we are feeling our most defeated and loneliest. Remember that you are not alone!

In the midst of every emotion, there is one constant.

God cares and is with you! God cares deeply about every emotion swirling in our hearts.

If you are on the mountaintop and feeling as if things couldn't be better, *God cares for you and is with you!*

If you are currently experiencing hurt or disappointment in ministry, remember this: *God cares and is always with you!*

God is close to you when you feel alone. He's close to you when you cry. He's close to you when you wonder how you'll move forward. Pour out your pain to God, and move closer to Him. The best news is, emotions are fleeting. We can choose how we direct our thoughts and energy. Instead of nursing our pain, we can find freedom in choosing to cling to our hope in God.

DON'T WALK, RUN TO HELP

If you're burned out, beat up, discouraged, depressed, hurting, or lonely, if your marriage is struggling, or if your schedule is controlling you instead of you controlling it, please get help. You can tell someone. Bring someone else into your pain and struggles. Talk to your spouse. Confide in a friend. Sit down with your pastor. Make an appointment with a counselor.

We've talked to so many leaders who say they just can't afford to get counseling. Perhaps it is a financial expense that you just can't scrape up out of your budget. Maybe you feel you can't afford the talking, the gossip, the rumors, or the ever-present eyes in the waiting room of the Christian counseling office.

But the truth is, you can't afford *not* to get help if you need it. Your family, your health, your marriage, and your ministry may hang in the balance. Not getting help isn't an option.

Do you trust God with your reputation? Do you trust Him with your calling? Do you trust Jesus with your relationships? Do you trust that God will do His part in healing you, if you are willing to step out and get help?

Find a Christian counselor who sees pastors and their families pro bono. Drive to a nearby town to step out of the spotlight. Ask whether a counselor will meet after office hours or over the phone. Travel to a counseling center that specializes in helping people in ministry. Find a way around the excuses that keep you from getting help. Too much is at stake. If you need help, please get it! Run after it.

Lying on a lumpy cot in a poorly lit cell in the psych ward, Heather was left with only her socks and her God. Stripped of her possessions, her relationships, and her freedom, she realized that no one could strip her of her faith if she was willing to desperately rely on Jesus. She stood face to face with God that night and committed to doing whatever He asked her to do to get healthy again.

For the next year, Heather became a student of God. With the help of weekly visits to a psychologist, prescription medication, and the wonderful support of her husband, Heather embarked on the incredibly difficult journey back to restoration and healing. She learned that before she was a pastor's wife, before she was a Bible study leader, she was a child of God. No matter what happened to those roles and that calling, she allowed God to restore her as His child.

Twelve years later, Heather faithfully serves the God Who put her back together, by living out the desperate faith she discovered that lonely, horrible night in the psych ward. A desperate faith that is willing to take any action to touch the untouchables, to befriend the friendless, and to help restore people as children of God.

CHAPTER 10

Change and Transition

I dread church and then feel guilty about re-
senting my role in all this.

Confession

MAY 2, 2010, started out as a normal, rainy spring
day in Nashville. Flowers were blooming, the grass was
the perfect springtime green, birds were chirping, and
the occasional frog croaked in my (Brandi's) backyard.
Our day was spent at the ballpark and planting in the
garden. Life was normal. Life was comfortable. We
were content.

Little did we know that thirty-six hours later our city
would be ravaged by flooding that wiped out homes,
businesses, and life as we knew it. In fact, several of
our staff members left their homes to go to work that
Sunday, and when they arrived back home four hours
later their homes were under nine feet of water or
filled with mud as the hills behind their homes col-

lapsed. When the rain stopped, over nine thousand homes and businesses were destroyed by floodwaters. Unfortunately, 90 percent of the homes destroyed were not covered by flood insurance, as the homes weren't anywhere close to the previously defined floodplain. Even as I write this two years later, there are still abandoned homes, destroyed by the flooding, that I drive past daily.

One day everything was gorgeous and engulfed in the beauty of spring, and the next day the city we love was destroyed. Friends were homeless; security vanished. Life, as previously known, no longer existed. We were in the midst of a change, a transition that none of us could have predicted. Our community looked very different. Friends were permanently changed. Hearts were broken, and tears were shed. Our church was overwhelmed, and our people were wrecked. Yet in the midst of the confusion and fear, we knew we were not alone. We knew, beyond a shadow of a doubt, that God was using each one of us during this time. He was shaping us, growing us, binding our hearts together and closer to Him.

We, as individuals and as a community, were devastated. But throughout our devastation, our hope was in knowing that God was doing a greater work. He was our constant.

Change is packaged in many different ways. We face change as we move from one season of life to the next. Sometimes we shift from one leadership position to another, and as excited as we are, it's still transition. Location changes can come when we least expect them. You're settled in a community you love, and you hear God calling you to another part of the country. And then some of us are called to transition whole organizations, to take a church from a style they've grown comfortable with and push them into the next period of ministry.

Obviously, change looks different for everyone, and we each handle it in our own unique way. But change is inevitable. Sometimes we choose the change, and sometimes change is chosen for us. Either way, it's usually a tricky circumstance to maneuver. Sometimes that maneuvering is smooth, like gliding across ice on a perfectly sharpened pair of skates, but more often it feels as if you're wading through waist-high muck, constantly trying to catch your breath.

We often don't like the time it takes to adjust to change and get in sync with transition. We're quick-aholics. We eat fast food and instantly download movies we used to have to wait months to find at our local video store. It's possible to have new jeans shipped to our house overnight and beam down a new book to an e-reader in sixty seconds.

We don't usually want to take the time to wait and see how something is going to turn out. Our culture has made us very uncomfortable with change and transition. We prefer to make things happen in our own time frame. While we know "God is with us" or "God has called us to this," we sometimes feel the loneliest in the midst of change and transition.

Many times, we must face change or transition to see that God is in control. He is there working in our lives at our darkest and loneliest points. Let's look at the life of Elijah, starting in 1 Kings 18. This is the story of Ahab, a fierce guy who worshipped idols and was bad to the bone.

God sends Elijah to announce that a drought is coming and a severe famine is going to ensue. Everyone ignores Elijah until three years have passed and there has been no rain. When we hit verse 20, Elijah, King Ahab, and 450 prophets of Baal are on Mount Carmel at an altar. A challenge is set forth that whoever can get their god to come down and bring fire on the sacrifice is the winner. Elijah is more than ready. He's so ready, he even starts to taunt them by covering his altar in twelve jars of water (obviously not optimal for burning conditions).

Then Elijah calls on God, and the Bible says that fire comes down and consumes Elijah's sacrifice. Consumes. Doesn't just torch it. Doesn't merely send a spark. God consumes Elijah's sacrifice. There is no doubt that Elijah did one heck of a victory dance after his God consumed the sacrifice.

We love victory, don't we? We love seeing God

dominate; watching God consume. We love chapters like 1 Kings 18. We believe we are made for chapters like 1 Kings 18.

Yet often we ignore chapters like the one immediately before. You can't fully appreciate chapter 18 until you fully understand chapter 17. Chapter 17 actually gives us insight into God's doing something miraculous for Elijah, setting the stage for victory. In chapter 17 God tells Elijah he can live like no one else. He is to go to the wilderness, where he'll be taken care of by birds that will feed him and he'll be able to drink from the brook. So Elijah, being obedient, does *what the Lord told him*. He goes to the wilderness and stays there. Birds bring him bread and meat in the morning and bread and meat in the evening, and he drinks from the cool brook.

Elijah was where God called him to be. He was smack-dab in the middle of some sort of odd change, a strange transition in his life. There are times when you'll be exactly where God wants you to be, doing what God has called you to do, and you might be vulnerable. You might not be comfortable. You might be lonely, anxious, or scared. Being in God's will is the right place, but not always the safest place.

You could be serving in a church God called you to, but it's not necessarily going to be safe. You might be launching a new ministry that, without a shadow of a doubt, God called you to launch, but it may not be comfortable. Maybe you're planting a church that God clearly gave you the vision for, but anxiety surrounds you. There are many times in our lives when we are going to be exactly where God called us to be, and it's not going to feel safe. Your desire to follow your Savior is the right thing, but it isn't always the easiest thing to do.

Back to Elijah. Chapter 17, verse 7, has huge significance in Elijah's life. *But after a while the brook dried up, for there was no rainfall anywhere in the land.* Wait?! The brook dried up?! The brook that was the source of Elijah's life, his source of hope, was bone-dry? Elijah must have been wondering, "God, what are You doing right now? You told me to come here, now what have You done?" And every day that passed without water, Elijah must have gotten more desperate.

During your change and transition you might be asking, "God, I thought You called us to move here." "God, I thought this whole following You thing would be different." "God, I thought You told us to take that position." "God, I thought You called me to marry him." You might feel as if your brook has dried up. You have been told your entire life that God is for you, yet you feel as if your brook is missing water. You believe God is gracious, but why is your brook more like a desert?

Often when our brooks dry up, we hear God most clearly. He needs our attention and surrender. He needs us to listen. Without chapter 17, Elijah would not have enjoyed the victory God provided in chapter 18 as much. Without the drought, Elijah wouldn't have felt joy that shook him to the depths of his soul. Without his desperation, he never would have felt the fullness God provides.

If we look back to chapter 17, we will see a promise being made: God is going to provide for Elijah. God promises that He will take care of Elijah's needs. When a promise is made, there are two parts that exist: the promiser and the promisee. The *responsibility* lies with the promiser. You are not the promiser. When our Savior compels you, you must go. You can't change your circumstances or the people around you; you can't even change you. Your job during your change and transition is to learn to trust the Promiser. Our natural tendency is to jump in and control, to manipulate the situation. If our churches aren't growing, our staff is in turmoil, our building program is behind budget, we aren't connecting to our new church, or our aging parents need more of our time, we try to manipulate and control those situations, when what we are really called to do is trust our Promiser. Trust the God who has called us to this moment.

As hard as times of change and transition are, following God and trusting Him are of the utmost importance. So let's take a very practical look at several different types of change: personal, professional, and church change.

PERSONAL CHANGE

A new season. When we each moved to Nashville and Vegas, we were both a whopping eight months pregnant. Jett was born four weeks after the Wilson move, and Ethan was born five weeks after the Wilhites started to unpack boxes. Both of us moved into new communities with swollen ankles, superfat fingers, and protruding bellies. We stepped into new roles, new babies, and new cities all at once. Talk about being lost. Looking back now, it was a miracle we survived those simultaneous changes and lived to tell about it.

Of all the transitions, adding a baby to the mix was the hardest. We desired growing families, and new babies bring so much joy. So why did we feel as if we were floundering?

Having infants and toddlers at home really changed our level of involvement in leadership. Maybe it is just us, but we don't get out much for a while after having a baby. Going to the grocery store can seem almost as impossible as scaling Mount Everest. Kids changed the way we did ministry. It wasn't bad; we love our children and wouldn't trade them for anything, but it was definitely a transition.

Maybe your personal change isn't bringing babies home from the hospital or adding a high chair to your kitchen table, but instead you're packing those babies up as you send them off to college. Maybe you are facing the personal transition of the empty nest. Or possibly you've reached the time when you are caring for aging parents either in town or in your home. You work during the day and are a caretaker in the evenings. You've hit a new season in your life.

It's important to redefine what ministry looks like for us during each new season. At the time, we believed that once we "redefined," it would stay that way for a while. Little did we know we would be redefining on a regular basis. There have been seasons when it's felt as if we were in constant transition, getting used to a certain practice only to find ourselves shifting once again. The key has been finding the groove that worked best for our family and for our giftings. There have been parenting seasons when we've said no to everything outside of family. Seasons when we've been clear that only two slots each month were allotted to personal outside activities. Seasons when we've called on friends and parents to lend extra support to our family. We've learned to be flexible, to be willing to shift and adjust in a way that allowed us to serve but also protected our families.

Each new season comes with a unique set of challenges, but it is also accompanied by its own set of strengths. The challenge is to find the strength of the season you are in. Amazingly, there are things you can only do when you have young kids at home. There are also certain leadership moments that can be better accomplished when you have teens than when you are an empty-nester. And there are ministry opportunities in which you can better serve when your kids are adults rather than when they're tiny. Search for and find the strength of the season God has you in now, and then serve Him to the best of your ability.

Recently we were faced with a realization, one that's kind of hard to swallow: we're not as young as we used to be. Ouch.

We used to look around our staff meetings feeling like babies...Pete and Brandi planting Cross Point when they were twenty-seven, and Jud and Lori taking over Central at thirty-one and twenty-seven. We were the young kids who were leading amazing teams, staffs, and churches. Now we look around those same rooms and, well, we don't look quite as young as before. With years and road miles behind us and young couples coming on board, we're certainly feeling our age.

It's a new season in our lives. We are now considered the "seasoned" pastors' wives, yet there are times when we both still feel like the newbies. Times when we feel unprepared to carry the load and extend advice and, dare we say, "wisdom."

So yes, it's a new season, making us feel a little more

"mature" than we'd like to feel. But we are both excited about being able to invest in another generation
the way we were each invested in. It's a reminder of
how honored we are to do what we get to do. As we
enter a season of investing in those around us, we both
realize we're still learning. We seek guidance from
those who have gone ahead of us, those who are in
the next season of life. As women, our lives are often defined by seasons, and those seasons don't apply
just to marriage and motherhood but also to ministry.
There will be seasons when you absorb more and seasons when you're invested at a deeper level. But each
season calls us to be students of Christ so that He can
help guide us through the many different changes and
transitions we will face.

PROFESSIONAL CHANGE

When you leave. Just as there are different personal
changes that come our way during our life journeys,
we'll encounter quite a few professional transitions as
well. What do you do when God is moving you on
to another ministry opportunity? How do we, as staff,
leave and transition well? Keep these practical things
in mind as you transition.

- **The way in which you leave will be the way you
  are remembered.** If you go out throwing mud, that
  is how the staff and peers are going to remember

you. Rather than fondly recalling all the years of ministry highs and the joys along the way, people can find that those memories, unfortunately, get tainted by the way church leaders leave.

- **Celebrate the good, let go of the bad.** Struggles, frustrations, and concerns are involved anytime people leave a ministry position. We can choose to focus on those negative things or choose to celebrate all the wonderful things God has done and is doing through that ministry. Our focus is incredibly important.

  This is a great time to have one-on-one meetings with people you have served, recognizing their strengths and all that you see God doing in and through them. What a great opportunity to affirm and encourage the people you've worked alongside.

- **Care more about the people than the job they do for the church.** Hang on to the love you have for those leaders. Don't burn bridges when you are leaving. Three or four years from now, you may need those bridges, friendships, and support in ministry. We've been so thankful to be able to help former staff members find new jobs and opportunities even years after they've left. That is part of the beauty of maintaining those bridges.

- **Be wise with your words; don't blow the church up on your way out.** Think about the effect your words are going to have on the people you love once you leave, even three to six months down the road. We've seen certain staff members through the years leave in such a way that the volunteers or friends they had while serving at the church have such a bad taste in their mouths about the church that they really struggle. In some of the worst, saddest cases... they leave church and are unwilling to attend anywhere. That isn't what any of us want for the people we love.

The questions will be asked: Why are you leaving? What's wrong? What has happened? Choose your words wisely. Remember that the people you are talking to are staying to serve at or attend the church. Remember that it will still be their church family and their church home. Protect them.

- **Attempt to maintain relationships,** especially in that first year. Reach out to your former coworkers, staff members, and leaders. We've heard many times, "No one from our old church has called us or reached out to us." Well, that goes both ways. Pick up the phone. E-mail them. Be proactive in keeping those relationships up. We obviously can't control the responses of others, but we can control ourselves and our actions.

- **Maintain your integrity.** Period. If gossip gets stirred up, or hurtful things are said, you hang on to your integrity no matter what. Do not, by your actions, hand your integrity over to anyone else.

There are mandates that we have in place for staff members. When we, as staff, leave, they should absolutely still be in effect.

Be loyal to leadership.

Leak up, not out. When there is a grievance about something, leak up to your supervisors and leaders, not out to your peers, volunteers, or church members. Again, care enough about the people staying to protect them from negative talk.

Follow Matthew 18. If the air needs to be cleared with another staff member or leader, go to them. Not to your buddies. Not to your coworkers. Go to the staff member or leader. Talk about it. Work it out.

Now is the time when some of you are thinking, "But there are some things that aren't right. There are things at the church that aren't working. I feel as if I need to bring those things to light." Here is the challenge. If you've resigned, it is no longer your job to do this. Do you believe that we have a big, big God who will bring all things to light in His time, not ours? We have certainly seen God bring things to light, and He, amazingly, didn't need our help to do it. Take those things to Him.

The big move. Oftentimes when there is a role transition, we also find ourselves in the midst of a move. We begin collecting cardboard boxes and whipping out the bubble wrap. We load up the U-Haul, leaving everything and everyone we are comfortable with, to follow God to a new city, a new church, a new adventure. While these are times of great excitement and anticipation, let's be honest, they are also times of heartbreaking good-byes, puffy red eyes, and loads of anxiety. Moving is a huge transition.

I (Brandi) am the epitome of a small-town girl. A small-town girl God chose to move to the big city! My hometown in Kentucky boasts a whopping four hundred bodies. Until age twenty-five, I existed in communities where I knew everyone and everyone knew me. Unlike most people, I loved that. There was comfort in being known. At twenty-five and pregnant, I was excited about our move to Nashville, but that move came with an immense amount of grief. I was leaving behind a job I loved, people I adored, and a town that housed familiar faces around every corner. God had worked in my heart; I knew Nashville was our next move, but it hurt so much to go through the steps of leaving what had been our only home.

There were significant cultural adjustments. We had to meet people and make new friends—all as typical with any move. I knew right away that a huge struggle for me would be relationships. I'm a people person and knew it would be important for me to connect with people as quickly as possible. Knowing I would need to be proactive, I didn't just sit around and wait for people to come to me.

Pretty quickly my small-town roots started to dig in and feel at home. I started seeing familiar faces in the grocery store and finding girlfriends I could meet for coffee. Soon the cultural differences started to fade as well. Nashville didn't seem quite as big; I could drive across town and make it back home without getting lost. God began to grow my heart for our city. He brought me friendships and created avenues where I could serve. He gifted me with "small-town" moments, helping me feel at home. I embraced my community with open arms. God focused my vision, blocking the negative stuff associated with a bigger city and bringing into focus ministry opportunity. Today, it can't be exaggerated how much Pete and I adore Nashville.

If you've recently moved or are staring down the barrel of a relocation, here are a few practical things that might help you in your transition.

- **Be proactive.** Don't sit in your home or apartment with the blinds drawn, hoping someone will call you for lunch or a movie night out. Get out there; make it happen. Start a book club. Ask some ladies to meet for coffee. Have some gals over to watch the *Downton Abbey* season premiere together. It doesn't really matter what you do, just do something. It is really difficult to meet people if you aren't willing to put yourself out there.

- **Ask God to give you a deep love for your city and the people He's called you to serve.** The culture may be different. Yes, the people may be unlike any you've ever seen. And you might not totally understand their strange accents. Allow God to turn your heart toward your community. He has brought you there for a purpose. He will mold your heart to embrace the community He has placed you in. Get to know your city, find favorite restaurants, stores, and places to take friends who visit. Becoming familiar with the uniqueness of your community will help you appreciate your surroundings all the more.

- **Give yourself time.** The friendships you spent five or ten years building will not be replaced within a few months. All relationships take time to develop and grow. Maintain friendships from your previous location; just because you move doesn't mean those friendships end. You'll probably have to get creative in communication and use those cell phone minutes or Skype one another, but it's okay to stay in contact with those people you were close to as you develop and grow new friendships.

New shoes to fill. At some point in the last sixteen years during which we've each been in ministry, our husbands have filled each of the following roles: youth pastor, college pastor, discipleship minister, director of ministries, teaching pastor, church planter, and senior pastor. With every role change, there has been adjustment. How did we fit? How could we serve alongside our husbands? What did ministry look like for us now?

We had to figure out how to be completely us—with all our craziness and screw-ups. You, too, will have to figure out how to be you in a new role. That transition can take much longer than you might expect. But bit by bit, slowly along the way, you'll grow into more of you. Even when we have both felt ourselves flailing in our roles, we've known that some of God's greatest lessons are taught in our flailing. Those seasons of figuring it out have often included our greatest personal growth.

The role transition to the senior pastor's wife just about kicked my (Lori's) booty. The additional time requirements for Jud really surprised me. I struggled with the relational differences with people in the church. I floundered around for a little while, trying to get comfortable in my new role. Everything just seemed so much more intense.

A few years ago Jud and I heard Dave Stone speaking about what he had learned since becoming the senior pastor of Southeast Christian Church in Louisville, Kentucky. He talked about all the things he had thought he knew or understood, and about how wrong he'd been. Oh my word, could I relate. Many times I've thought I should go back and apologize to our former senior pastors because I thought they should have handled something differently, didn't have a clue, or should have done something better.

One of the things Dave talked about was leadership being like the layers of an onion. As his level of leadership changed, he moved more and more toward the outer layers of the onion. He hadn't realized that while he had been leading in his various roles, he was being protected by the outer layer of that onion, the senior pastor. There were many complaints, criticisms, and ugliness that never hit his desktop because they had been absorbed by the senior pastor. Once he became that outer layer, well, he saw things in a whole new light. He had become, as the senior pastor, an outer layer of protection for his staff, the volunteers, and the church.[1]

We (Lori and Brandi) personally did not have the ability to understand the weight the senior pastor and his wife carried in leadership and ministry until we were in that role ourselves. We don't share this story to extend condemnation, as we're both senior pastors' wives, but to help explain the weight that is carried in *all* levels of leadership.

If you are frustrated with the leadership around

you, hit Pause and extend some grace to them. Odds are that you have no idea what they are shouldering or what layers of protection they provide for you. You may have no clue how hard it is to walk in their shoes. Pray for them. Encourage them. Someday you may stand in their shoes, and we hope you have others who are willing to lift you up as well.

When staff leaves. What about when we are the ones being left? A coworker or leader has decided to leave the church. What then? Having staff leave your church or organization can be an emotional, intense experience, but it doesn't have to be negative.

There are several things to keep in mind when staff are planning to leave or are announcing that they are leaving:

- **Leaving is not betrayal.** Oh, sure, sometimes ugly things can go down with the way in which some people leave. But the actual leaving, or interviewing, is not betrayal. It isn't necessarily a personal hit or a poor reflection on your leadership.

  If God is calling staff to another job or another ministry, that isn't a bad thing. Following the call of God is an amazing thing. None of us want staff who ignore or disobey the call of God in some misguided display of loyalty. Instead of being hurt, let's cheer them on and encourage them as they follow God's leading in their lives.

- **Again, care more about your people than the job they do for the church.** There are two church cultures you can create when it comes to this issue. You can create a culture of fear or a culture of caring. A culture of fear forces staff to look at other ministry opportunities in secret. A culture that cares more about people than their job allows them to openly discuss and journey with you as they are seeking God and new opportunities.

We've had the honor of praying for, advising, listening to, and journeying with lots of staff members who have felt God moving them on to other ministries. It is a privilege to encourage someone as they are seeking God and following Him.

- **Celebrate.** Celebrate the work the staff has done in ministry. Celebrate their time with the church. Celebrate the new adventure God is calling them to. Celebrate their willingness to follow God. Just celebrate.

One of the best pieces of advice we have received about navigating through staff leaving came from a fellow pastor's wife. When asked how her church handles a staff member's choosing to leave, she passed along words of wisdom that have stuck with us. She said honestly that in the past she'd taken it personally and been hurt when staff had chosen to leave. But over the years she has come to look at a departing staff member's time at their church as an investment. The staff member has been "in training" while on their staff for some God-ordained purpose, and when they choose to leave, it is because God has moved them somewhere else to minister. The church has been lucky to be part of the staff member's experiences and part of their journey. As staff leaves, you must remember that an experience is never wasted. So celebrate getting to be part of their journey in ministry.

NKOTB. Remember Donnie, Danny, Joey, Jordan, and Jonathan? The New Kids on the Block. If not, then we probably seem very ancient to you now, but think *NSYNC, Backstreet Boys, Menudo, the Jackson 5, and the Jonas Brothers. You know, a good old-fashioned singing and dancing boy band. We had NKOTB posters on our walls, kept their pins on our acid-washed denim jackets, and could do a mean version of the "Hangin' Tough" dance. There is another kind of New Kid on the Block who doesn't require amazing hair and droves of screaming, crying teenage girls. Anytime you have a leadership transition, you are dealing with the new kid on the block.

When Jud and I (Lori) came to Central, we took over for a much-loved pastor who had been at the church for eighteen years. The day we moved in, Jud said, "Don't unpack all the boxes. We might not make it." We had seen plenty of other pastors come into similar situations and end up being transition pastors, easing the way for the next guy.

I'll admit, the first couple of years were bumpy—they reminded me of when I was a little girl and my aunt would drive so fast over road bumps that my tiny eight-year-old body would fly out of the seat and I'd hit my head on the roof of her big conversion van. Yep, that kind of bumpy. One thing someone told us about, and I was so grateful for this wisdom, was the progression of people deciding whether they are going to follow a new leader.

The first group is the crowd. These are the people who attend church semiregularly. They decide right away whether they will stay or go. For us, this absolutely turned out to be true. After we showed up, our attendance quickly dropped about 20 percent. There was a good-sized section of the crowd who weren't interested in the new kids on the block.

The second group is the congregation. These are your regular attendees who aren't superinvolved in the life of the church. Our friend told us that the congregation makes its decision about a leader around the one-year mark. The third group of people is the core, who hold out for about two years before they make their decision. They love the church and are very involved. They are also incredibly committed to the previous vision of the church. When people in this group decide to leave, it's probably the most painful.

We certainly felt those three waves of people and saw groups leave at those times. It is hard to see people leave the church. It is sad to watch the board who hired you leave to attend somewhere else. It is difficult to hear accusations that you are ruining the church because change is taking place. God has always been good to us in this respect and used the extra space to help us reach more people. Having people leave is hurtful, but it is also part of a leadership transition.

CHURCH CHANGE

Both of our churches have gone through major transitions: from changing styles to launching new campuses. From staff expansions to building projects. Regardless of what kind of organization or ministry you lead, change will occur. The majority of the time, excitement accompanies change; we function full of anticipation, ready to tackle the hurdles.

Through change, we have prayed for protection and endurance, guidance and wisdom. Those are powerful prayers. But in the midst of transition, tears are often shed. Tears over the introduction of those loud drums and guitars. Tears over not seeing the same friends they've seen every week for the past twenty years. Tears over the loss of the way things "used to be." Tears because they just don't like change. At all. Often our first instinct is to remind our teary-eyed members of the vision of the church, how we know God has called us to take this step, that this is a great thing.

But one thing we've come to realize about ministry is the need to allow people to *feel*. It's not always our job to make sure they're on board with our vision; there is an appropriate time for that, but there's also a need to let people work through their emotions, to respond to change. In order to move forward into a healthy environment, emotions should be processed, and it's acceptable for feelings to be justified. So when you're walking your church or your team through those pains of change, remember to allow them to *feel*.

Then refocus and fully embrace the vision that God has called your church to follow. There will be some people who will never be able to move past hurt feelings and grief over losing the way things used to be. That is okay. They may move on to new church homes and ministries. It is sad, but it happens. As leaders, though, it is vital that we stay committed to God's vision for our ministries. We must stay sold-out to His vision above all else—above feelings and fears.

Regardless of where you are in your change or transition, you must remember that He is your constant. The Promiser of all things has made a promise to you.

And just as He took care of Elijah, He will take care of you. He will provide for you. Your circumstances might seem impossible; you might want to jump ship, but your job in the midst of your change is to remember to trust the Promiser.

Loving It

WE THINK THE "typical" pastor's wife or woman in ministry is dead. You know, that woman who had it all together, never seemed to struggle, played the piano, attended every event, and met everyone's expectations—although she could have had some help with her wardrobe.

We've heard, read, and said "I'm not the typical pastor's wife" so many times, we've started to wonder if she really ever existed at all, or if she really only existed in people's minds and expectations.

We spend mass amounts of time, energy, emotion, and effort comparing ourselves to a myth. And the problem is—we fall short. Our attention turns to our shortcomings and failings instead of staying focused on God and who He created us to be.

But the truth is, God knew exactly what He was doing, exactly who He was calling. He knows our short-comings and our struggles, and He has extended His call to leadership and ministry anyway.

Maybe "typical" isn't what we thought. Maybe there is a new typical. Maybe we are typical. The more we talk to pastors' wives and women in ministry, the more we realize how alike we are.

Regardless of age, location, denomination, church style, or church size, we all have the same questions, struggles, and difficulties.

It is time to embrace the knowledge that maybe we *are* typical—women wanting to know Jesus, support our husbands, love our children, care for our churches, and grow in love and grace.

We find peace as we cling to Him in times of challenge—wrestling with our own shortcomings, keeping our heads up during the tough times, ac-knowledging that we won't be all things to all people, yet making ourselves available to fellow strugglers.

As women in leadership, we learn to trust the Sovereignty of the Almighty God, Who has called us to partner with Him in His work—finding purpose in our unique giftedness, comfort in knowing He doesn't make mistakes, and rest as we embrace who He made us to be.

We are not perfect. But we may well be typical, and that is fine by us. The truth is, God could use anyone...*any*one...to accomplish His mission. But He gives us, and He gives you, the honor and privilege of getting to be part of His work. You never know who God is drawing to Himself and who He has pulled into the seats of your church. Always remember the calling God has put on your life, to connect the unconnected with Christ.

There is great joy in following God's calling on our lives. As you lead:

Remember, life-giving community is necessary. We could talk until we're blue in the face about the importance of life-giving community; we believe it is that important. Sometimes we're blessed to find friendships that feed us within our ministry communities. And sometimes we have to step back and widen our friendship horizons.

Doing ministry in the twenty-first century has a lot of advantages—for example, our ability to connect with people who aren't in our own city or even in the same state. We live in an age of technology that allows us to connect easily with those who are geographically far away. Our ministry at Leading and Loving It (leadingandlovingit.com) offers virtual and local community groups for pastors' wives and women in ministry. Community groups are exactly what they sound like; they're women connecting in small-group formats, virtually or in person, just like those in your churches and ministries. We cannot encourage you enough to take advantage of that ability to connect with others. Jump in. Join the Leading and Loving It community. Find connection in community groups, encouragement in the daily blog posts, and support at retreats and virtual conferences.

Remember to love extravagantly. In 1 Corinthians 13, Paul says: *If I could speak all the languages of earth and of angels, but didn't love others, I would only be a noisy gong or a clanging cymbal. If I had the gift of prophecy, and if I understood all of God's secret plans and possessed all knowledge, and if I had such faith that I could move mountains, but didn't love others, I would be nothing.*[1] Regardless of what ministries we create, what jobs we take, or which organization we lead, it all boils down to loving others well.

Great Bible studies or messages will get us pats on the back. Savvy leadership skills will win admiration from colleagues. Hard work will catch people's eyes.

But if we don't love, we're nothing more than a noisy gong or a clanging cymbal. If we don't love the people God has placed in our lives, nothing else really matters. Love them in their brokenness. Love them in their messiness. Love them in their desperation. Love them when they are hurting and when they hurt you. Love them when they finally intersect with God's hope, grace, love, acceptance, and forgiveness.

Lead, and love it.

Notes

CHAPTER 1

1. NIV.
2. Jessica Cornelius, "JustONE Conference," LeadingandLovingIt.com (January 2012, recorded video, http://leadingandlovingit.com/media/).
3. 1 Thessalonians 3:11 (MSG).
4. B. B. Warfield, *The Person and Work of Christ,* ed. Samuel G. Craig (Philadelphia: Presbyterian & Reformed Publishing, 1950), 96.
5. MSG.
6. Kay Warren, "Private Lives of Public People," Saddleback Church, Lake Forest, CA (2011, recorded message).
7. Linda Seidler, "Authenticity vs. Trans-

parency," SharpenHer, Tricia Lovejoy
(October 19, 2011, http://sharpenher.com/).

CHAPTER 2

1. Gloria Steinem, "Gloria Steinem Quotes,"
   BrainyQuote, BookRags Media Network
   (2012, www.brainyquote.com/quotes/
   authors/g/gloria_steinem.html).
2. Beth Moore, *Between Us—Ministers' Wives,* A
   Lifeway Event (March 2009, paraphrased
   from an unrecorded live talk).
3. NIRV.
4. Kay Warren, "Private Lives of Public People,"
   Saddleback Church, Lake Forest, CA (2011,
   recorded message).
5. Heather Palacios, "This Is My Battlefield…
   Maybe It's Yours," LeadingandLovingIt.com,
   (July 13, 2011, http://leadingandlovingit.com/
   leadership/this-is-my-battlefield-maybe-its-
   yours-2/).

CHAPTER 3

1. Holly Furtick, "I Can't Ride His Spiritual
   Coat-Tails," LeadingandLovingIt.com (July
   17, 2011, http://leadingandlovingit.com/
   spiritual-growth/i-cant-ride-his-spiritual-coat-
   tails/).
2. MSG.

3. Lisa Hughes, "JustONE Conference," LeadingandLovingIt.com (January 2012, recorded video, http://leadingandlovingit. com/media/).

4. John Ortberg, *The Me I Want to Be* (Grand Rapids: Zondervan, 2010).

5. Tiffany Cooper, "A Great Church," Leading andLovingIt.com (June 17, 2010, http:// leadingandlovingit.com/expectations/a-great-church/).

6. Lynn Hybels, *Nice Girls Don't Change the World* (Grand Rapids: Zondervan, 2005).

CHAPTER 4

1. Oswald Chambers, *My Utmost for His Highest* (Grand Rapids: Discovery House Publishing, 2010; Amazon Digital Services, 2011).

2. Quentin Fottrell, "Does Facebook Wreck Marriages?", Smart Money.com (May 21, 2012, http://blogs.smartmoney.com/advice/ 2012/05/21/does-facebook-wreck-marriages/).

3. Steve and Cindy Wright. "Ruth Graham—Finishing Well." *Marriage Missions International*. 26 2012: n. page. (Web. 4 Jan. 2013. http://www.marriagemissions.com/ ruth-graham—finishing-well-marriage-message-309/).

4. Natalie Witcher, "Forty Day Prayer Chal-

lenge," LeadingandLovingIt.com (May 2012, http://leadingandlovingit.com/resources/).

5. Shaunti Feldhahn, *For Women Only* (Sisters, OR: Multnomah Books, August 19, 2004; Random House Digital, 2010).

6. Linda Dillow, *What's It Like to Be Married to Me?* (Colorado Springs: David C Cook, 2011; Amazon Digital Services, 2011).

7. Linda Dillow, *What's It Like to Be Married to Me?* (Colorado Springs: David C Cook, 2011; Amazon Digital Services, 2011), 59.

CHAPTER 5

1. Tiffany Cooper, "Oozing with Wisdom, the PK Life," LeadingandLovingIt.com (January 27, 2011, http://leadingandlovingit.com/page/2/?s=julie+richard&x=0&y=0).

2. Tiffany Cooper, "Kids and Church," LeadingandLovingIt.com (June 9, 2011, http://leadingandlovingit.com/family/kids-church/).

3. Melissa Elswick, "JustONE Conference," LeadingandLovingIt.com (January 2012, recorded video, http://leadingandlovingit.com/media/).

CHAPTER 6

1. Holly Furtick, "You Asked...Mentors—Holly Furtick," HollyFurtick.com

(October 6, 2009, http://hollyfurtick.com/
you-asked-mentors/).

2. 2 Corinthians 6:11 (NIV).

3. Kay Warren, Catalyst West Luncheon,
LeadingandLovingIt.com (March 2010,
http://leadingandlovingit.com/media/).

4. MSG.

5. Kerri Weems, "JustONE Conference,"
LeadingandLovingIt.com (January 2012,
recorded video, http://leadingandlovingit.
com/media/).

6. Beth Moore, *Jesus—90 Days with the One and
Only* (Nashville: B&H Books, 2007; Amazon
Digital Services, 2010).

7. Curtis Sittenfeld, *American Wife* (New York:
Random House, 2008; Random House Digital, 2010), Chapter 17.

8. Simon Cowell, "Simon Cowell Quotes." *Brainy
Quotes* n.pag. *Brainy Quotes*. Web. (4 Jan
2013. http://www.brainyquote.com/quotes/au-
thors/s/simon_cowell.html).

9. Carmine Gallo. "The Management Wisdom
of Simon Cowell." *Forbes*. 04 2011: n. page.
Web. (4 Jan. 2013. http://www.forbes.com/
sites/carminegallo/2011/04/08/the-
management-wisdom-of-simon-cowell/).

CHAPTER 7

1. Sarah Young, *Jesus Calling* (Nashville: Thomas Nelson, 2004), 180.

2. Lisa Hughes, "JustONE Conference," LeadingandLovingIt.com (January 2012, recorded video, http://leadingandlovingit.com/media/).

3. Kerri Weems, "Creating Margin—Part 2," LeadingandLovingIt.com (August 3, 2011, http://leadingandlovingit.com/time/creating-margin-part-2/).

4. Kerri Weems, "JustONE Conference," LeadingandLovingIt.com, (January2012, recorded video, http://leadingandlovingit.com/media/).

5. Dan Allender, *Sabbath—The Ancient Practices* (Nashville: Thomas Nelson, 2009; Amazon Digital Services, 2010), 12.

6. Rick Warren, Catalyst West Conference, LeadingandLovingIt.com (April 24, 2009, http://leadingandlovingit.com/leadership/catalyst-west-rick-warren/).

7. Kay Warren, Catalyst West Luncheon, LeadingandLovingIt.com (March 2010, http://leadingandlovingit.com/media/).

CHAPTER 8

1. Tricia Lovejoy, SharpenHer.Com, Critics and

Critiques (April 13, 2011, http://sharpenher.
com/).

2. Kerri Weems, "The 'B' Word," Ker-
riWeems.com (April 28, 2011,
http://kerriweems.com/2011/04/28/pastors-
wives-the-b-word-3/).

3. Richard Rohr, *The Naked Now* (The Crossroad
Publishing Company, 2009).

4. Isaiah 41:13.

5. Andy Stanley, Catalyst Conference, Day 2,
Session 11 (Atlanta, October 8, 2010).

6. MSG.

7. Linda Dillow, *Calm My Anxious Heart*
(Colorado Springs: NavPress, 2010), 79.

8. Kyle Anderson, "Taylor Swift battles bullies,
critics, and silent movie villains in new 'Mean'
video," ew.com. 09 2011: n. page. Web. (4
Jan. 2013. http://music-mix.ew.com/2011/05/
09/taylor-swift-mean-video/).

CHAPTER 9

1. Tiffany Cooper, "Oozing with Wisdom—the
PK Life," LeadingandLovingIt.com (January
27, 2011, http://leadingandlovingit.com/page/
2/?s=julie+richard&x=0&y=0).

2. Tom Holladay, "Elijah: Becoming a Significant Servant," Saddleback Church Message
Archives (1995).

3. Donna Bordelon Alder, "How to Encourage Your Pastor's Wife," Thriving Pastor.org (2005, www.thrivingpastor.org/articles/married/A000000065.cfm).

4. D. Martyn Lloyd-Jones, *Spiritual Depression: Its Causes and Cures* (Grand Rapids: Eerdmans, 1965; Kindle Edition).

CHAPTER 10

1. Lori Wilhite, "The Onion—Dave Stone," LeadingandLovingIt.com (May 19, 2011, http://leadingandlovingit.com/leadership/the-onion-2/; paraphrased from an unrecorded live talk).

LOVING IT

1. 1 Corinthians 13: 1–2.